How To Make Money Online

Work From Home
and
Get Rich On The Internet

By Eric Borgos

Published By:
Impulse Communications, Inc.
14525 SW Millikan #56742
Beaverton, OR 97005
www.impulsecorp.com

Terms and Conditions:

No part of this book may be reproduced in any form or by any electronic or mechanical means, including information storage and retrieval systems, without written permission from the author, except in the case of a reviewer, who may quote brief passages embodied in critical articles or in a review.

Trademarked names appear throughout this book. Rather than use a trademark symbol with every occurrence of a trademarked name, names are used in an editorial fashion, with no intention of infringement of the respective owner's trademark.

The information in this book is distributed on an "as is" basis, without warranty. Although every precaution has been taken in the preparation of this work, neither the author nor the publisher shall have any liability to any person or entity with respect to any loss or damage caused or alleged to be caused directly or indirectly by the information contained in this book. All rights reserved.

Copyright 2015 © Eric Borgos

Dedication:

In loving memory of my grandfather, George L. Price, DDS, who introduced me to the world of finance at a very young age and mentored me as I grew older. His words of wisdom and support were invaluable to making me into the businessman I am today.

Table of Contents

Preface...1
How To Make Money Online.................................6
Why I Bought A Flower Store..............................14
Domain Flipping..20
The Story of DigiCredit.com................................25
Web Hosting Sucks...29
How I Invented A Plush Toy................................33
Working From Home..35
The Psychology of a Multi-Million Dollar Sale...............37
Publicity: Does It Bring Fame and Fortune?....................44
My Human-Powered Search Engine........................47
Sharing..50
Are Website Makeovers Worth It?......................52
Taking Your Business To The Next Level................56
My First Date..61
Domain Development..63
How My Web Host Screwed Me Out of $5,000.............71
Seller's Remorse...74
My Outsourcing Adventure.................................76
Illegal Sites...81
Amazon Mechanical Turk....................................86
Fake Passwords..88
What Is The Next Big Thing?..............................90
Bitcoin 2.0..94
Flipping Websites...98
Viral Videos (The Story of "Pimp My Sleigh").............101
Partnerships..105
Partnerships – Part II..108
Partnerships – Part III...110
SantaBot is Coming To Town............................115
How A Domain Name Sale Works....................118
Some Bitcoin 2.0 Business Ideas.......................122
Why I Am Happy To Sell At A Loss.................125
My Paperless Life...127

Dedication:

In loving memory of my grandfather, George L. Price, DDS, who introduced me to the world of finance at a very young age and mentored me as I grew older. His words of wisdom and support were invaluable to making me into the businessman I am today.

Table of Contents

Preface..1
How To Make Money Online.................................6
Why I Bought A Flower Store.............................14
Domain Flipping...20
The Story of DigiCredit.com..............................25
Web Hosting Sucks..29
How I Invented A Plush Toy...............................33
Working From Home...35
The Psychology of a Multi-Million Dollar Sale................37
Publicity: Does It Bring Fame and Fortune?...................44
My Human-Powered Search Engine...................47
Sharing...50
Are Website Makeovers Worth It?....................52
Taking Your Business To The Next Level........56
My First Date..61
Domain Development..63
How My Web Host Screwed Me Out of $5,000.............71
Seller's Remorse...74
My Outsourcing Adventure.................................76
Illegal Sites..81
Amazon Mechanical Turk...................................86
Fake Passwords..88
What Is The Next Big Thing?.............................90
Bitcoin 2.0..94
Flipping Websites...98
Viral Videos (The Story of "Pimp My Sleigh")...........101
Partnerships...105
Partnerships – Part II...108
Partnerships – Part III.......................................110
SantaBot is Coming To Town...........................115
How A Domain Name Sale Works..................118
Some Bitcoin 2.0 Business Ideas.....................122
Why I Am Happy To Sell At A Loss...............125
My Paperless Life..127

Some Websites Are Just Not Worth It..............................131
Buying Cheap Traffic..136
How I Was Scammed Out of $2,000..................................139
Striking It Rich With Bitcoin Cloud Mining..................145
My First Kiss..151
Giving Away My New Business Ideas.............................154
There Is Nothing New Anymore.......................................161
Mistakes and Failures...165
How I Found My Voice..169
Epilogue...172

Preface

The great thing about starting an Internet business is that there is always the potential to make millions of dollars. Paypal sold for $1.5 billion, Instagram for $1 billion, Nest for $3.2 billion, and Whatsapp for $19 billion. Even more amazing is that all these companies accomplished this within a few years of launching.

In contrast, if you open a traditional store, restaurant, or office it will most likely go out of business in the first few years, and even if it manages to survive you will probably just make enough money to live on. With websites, it's a whole different ballgame. The costs are so much lower, and the Internet is growing at such a fast rate, that it is hard not to make money.

The crazy part is you don't even have to make a profit to get rich. Youtube.com was purchased by Google for $1.65 billion, even though it was losing millions of dollars a month (from the video hosting costs), and many other companies have huge valuations even though they make no money. All that really seems to matter is that you build a site that gets a lot of visitors.

Even if people tell you your idea is stupid, there is still a decent chance you will succeed. It is very hard to predict which sites will make it and which won't. Who would have thought selling shoes online (without trying them on first) would be big business? But, e-store Zappos.com was purchased by Amazon.com for over $900 million.

I have found that there are two types of people looking to start an Internet business. Some have seen all the money companies like Google and Facebook are making and want to grab their fair share. With a business plan in hand, they are looking for investors so they can build a giant company. Other people want to start a home business or small office to try to make enough to live on. Maybe they don't like working for other people, don't like working in an office, want the opportunity to make more money, or can't find a decent job. Or, maybe they have a good business idea and decide to give it a try while they are in school or working at their existing job.

Whatever your goals are, the important part is just getting things started, no matter how you do it. Once you get your site launched, you will have a much better idea of its profit potential and what needs to be done to make it a success. Too many people waste months or years planning how to start their online business when instead they could have just set up a simple version of their site and then seen the response. Many times I have thought of a business idea and had it up and running the next day.

One reason many aspiring web entrepreneurs take so long to launch their business is they don't know how to do everything that needs to be done. There are many pieces of the puzzle, and without knowing about all of them, it is hard to get anywhere. My book will give you the information you need to get started, and the confidence to feel like you know what you are doing.

Part of feeling comfortable running your own Internet company is knowing more than just the practical aspects of your business. You will eventually be exposed to all sorts of opportunities, and to handle them correctly it helps to know as much as possible about a wide variety of business topics. After a few years, you can get this confidence through on-the-job experience, but hopefully my book will help give you a head start. I have launched hundreds of websites in all different areas of business, so the stories about my successes and failures are a good overview of the kind of ventures you may come across in cyberspace.

You might say to yourself all of this sounds interesting, but you really just want to open an online vitamin store (for example), so all you need to know is what it takes to sell vitamins online. Keep in mind, though, that Amazon.com started out in the book business, but now sells millions of items, and much of what they do relates more to the warehousing and distribution business than to any particular industry. Even Google is no longer just a search engine like back when they first started. Their main business is advertising, and they are also in many other markets such as cell phones, browsers, and self-driving cars. To be a success on the web, you can't only know about your little niche, you need to know a little of everything.

Another factor that holds people back when starting their business is a lack of money. Building a big business is very expensive, but I can show you how to get a small business started for almost nothing. So, cross that excuse off your list. If your small business goes well, you can then use your initial profits to expand, or you can search for investors and at least have a real website and a track record to show them.

One reason that running an Internet company remains a mystery to many people is that most business books are written from the perspective of creating and running a large company. They talk about business plans, venture capital, hiring and firing, managing, meetings, IPOs, business trips, and all the proper things that need to be handled when you become big. That is great information to know and plan for, but even Facebook or Google had to have a working website before they started worrying about any of this. So, it is my recommendation that no matter what your long term goals are, the most important thing is just to dive in head first and get your site launched.

In addition, if you read enough of the best-selling business books, you will eventually notice that for every book that says to do things one way, there is almost always another book saying to do the exact opposite. For every Donald Trump type tycoon, there are dozens of other real estate investors who got rich using completely different methods. Warren Buffet and Richard Branson have both made billions creating huge conglomerate corporations, but their stories are in no way alike. On top of that, much of what is written in famous business books does not even apply to the Internet. The Web has totally changed the entire dynamics of doing business. It is not that there is anything bad about the success strategies proposed by the leading wealth gurus; the problem is that these books lead the reader to think that there is only one right way to do things.

My own story is not a roadmap for you to follow on how to be successful; it is just one of the many paths an entrepreneur can take. What I show you in this book is that you can get rich no matter how you run your business. For example, as crazy as it sounds, I own a very profitable multi-million dollar Internet company where I:

- Never met any of the people who work for me.
- Bought 2 retail flower stores thousands of miles away from me without visiting them first or knowing anything about the flower business (or even how to run a store).
- Opened an office, but never once went to it.
- Tried to go public on the stock exchange, through a reverse merger.

- Never had a business plan.
- Bought and sold hundreds of websites, all without ever meeting the people I was dealing with.
- Never used a lawyer.
- Had my sites mentioned in the *Wall Street Journal*, *USA Today*, *Popular Science*, *Entrepreneur*, *Readers Digest*, and *Inc. Magazine*, as well as numerous radio and TV shows.
- Never have been to any industry conferences or trade shows.
- Invented a toy that was sold in Toys"R"Us.

Then, after 12 years of running my unconventional business, I sold half of my sites for $4.5 million to a buyer whom I never met and only spoke with once by phone.

The point of this book though is not about how I got rich. What follows is a combination of practical advice (names of websites and companies you can actually use to help launch your business) and tales of my most interesting business adventures. Together this will help give you the knowledge and confidence to blaze your own trail on the web. It is time for you to finally start making millions instead of just dreaming about it.

How To Make Money Online

Because I run my own Internet company, I often get asked the best way to make money online. Oddly enough, I have no good answer to that question. I was successful mostly because I got in on the ground floor (back in 1995). I started by creating web pages for small businesses for $50-$100 each, plus I offered hosting for them. Although being a web designer allowed me to run my own business from home, I still was paid hourly and had the pressure of constantly trying to get new customers. For a few weeks, I even hired somebody to do telemarketing for me for $10/hour. He did not own a computer and had never even been on the Internet, but he would randomly call local companies from the Yellow Pages and ask them if they were interested in putting their business online. If they expressed an interest, I would call them back and close the deal. This actually worked pretty well, but back then most small businesses did not want to spend much money on building a site. I eventually decided it was not worth the time and effort to convince people to create websites, just for the small amount of money I would make from it.

I also ran several online directories (this was before Yahoo and Google were around), where I charged people $20/month to advertise their website. One directory was for inventors (inventing.com), and the other was for multi-level marketers (cashflow.com). Most inventors and multi-level marketers did not have websites, so to get listed in my directory, they paid me an additional fee to build and host a web page for them. I was able to get a steady flow of customers from this, but the problem was that most inventors and multi-level marketers were very frugal. It was a big task for me each month to try to collect the $20/month. Only around half of them ended up paying, although it cost me nothing to run the sites, so it was all profit for me.

After a few years of being a web designer and web host, I saw all the sales my clients were getting from the pages I made for them. I decided I would be better off creating sites for myself instead. By then I had built up a portfolio of several hundred domain names, all of which were sitting there unused, so I decided to develop them. I bought some by doing what is now known as drop catching, which is buying domains right after they expire (when the owner does not pay the bill). There was no exact science to doing this, but I used to sit around and type really good domains into my browser, and if I saw the domain did not work, I would assume it was because the bill was unpaid. I would then look up the domain in the WHOIS system and see if it was past due. If it was, I would add it to my list. Each morning I would check all the domains on my list to see if they were suddenly available, and if one was, I would grab it. Network Solutions used to take the domains back around 4am-5am (Eastern Time) each morning, so I would make sure to get up by then and frantically type in my list of domains one by one to try to buy them. That is how I bought Bored.com. I also would sometimes find good domains that nobody ever registered before. For example, I remember trying to decide between buying MtEverest.com and MountEverest.com. I chose the shorter version, but I should have bought both.

Domain parking companies did not exist at that time, so I set up my own parking type pages, where I found a bunch of relevant links for a domain and listed them on one page. It was like a page of Google search results, but before Google was around. I then would add a few affiliate links to the top of each page, if I could find any related to that topic. The domains did well in the search engines, but there were so few affiliate programs back then that it was hard to make much money from it.

I decided to try something a little different with Bored.com. People were always asking me for links to good sites, so I decided to make a list of them on Bored.com, and that way I could just tell people to go there to find links they would like. I started with only 5-10 links, but once Bored.com started getting popular, I would add a few new links every month. The site did not make any significant money because there were no ad networks back then that I could use, and I didn't want to deal with selling ads myself. In the early 2000's, I was able to find some affiliate programs that were a good fit for the site (like free offers and contests, as bored people tend be interested in things like that), and Bored.com began making a few thousand dollars a month.

As the Internet grew in the early 2000's, so did the number of visitors to Bored.com, and I was able to run ads from major ad networks. As a result, income increased significantly, and I decided that instead of linking to other sites and giving them all the free traffic and ad income, I would be better off creating my own sites to link to instead. This also solved another problem I had, which was that sites I linked to would frequently go out of business, be offline temporarily due to server problems, or change their content so it would no longer be appropriate for me to link to. The only downside was that I had previously only spent a few hours a month running Bored.com, and it cost me nothing to run it. Building my own sites took a lot of time, and I had to hire programmers for it. I started off paying a programmer in Texas $65/hr to do the work for me, and he was great, but over the years I was able to find overseas programmers in places like Romania and India to do the same work for $5-$10/hr. Even some college students in the USA were willing to work for that price, so eventually I had around five programmers, a full-time web designer, and a few other people doing various projects. This allowed me to come out with 5-10 new sites every month to add to Bored.com, and each of these sites earned additional money because they had the built-in traffic from Bored.com. The sites also would get their own search engines listings, bringing more traffic to Bored.com. By 2007, Bored.com was getting around 70,000 visitors per day and making a profit of around $35,000/month.

The only problem with all of this was that in addition to running Bored.com, I also had dozens of other sites to run, had to manage all the workers, and deal with constant hassles of running a business (paying bills, payroll, insurance, phone calls, emails, servers, customer service, contracts, taxes, etc.). After ten years of doing this 7 days a week, I decided to sell Bored.com. I ended up selling it, along with 170 related sites, for $4.5 million ($3 million after the broker's commission and income taxes) in 2008.

In the next five years, I sold almost all of my 9,000 unused domain names for $3 million. Although I was making around $250,000 a year selling 50-100 of these domains, I was quickly running out of good ones to sell. I also worried domains would become less valuable over time due to the planned introduction of thousands of new domain extensions, as well as the shift in user behavior to mobile devices and social networks (where domains are not as relevant).

So, that is the story of how I made money online. Other than my old sites, almost none of the sites I created or bought in the past few years have made any significant money. It may be because I didn't promote them well, but I think it is much harder to get a good site noticed nowadays. That is not to say you can't make money online though. There are plenty of people who recently started sites that became successful. The good news is that it is much easier, faster, and cheaper to start a website than it ever was. It is certainly worth trying any ideas you have because you never know what will catch on.

Now back to my advice on how to get rich online. Much like how I started Bored.com or went on a domain buying binge in the 1990s, sometimes you just have to take a chance to try something, anything at all. Start small. Don't spend a year getting everything set up, don't spend months writing a business plan, don't go looking for financing. Just do some version of it. Your crazy idea could end up making a lot of money. You can't get rich if you aren't even in the game.

If you are not sure what to do, here are some ideas to help get you started:

Sell A New Product - Invent something and sell it on a crowdfunding site such as Kickstarter.com, Indiegogo.com, and Fundable.com. The amazing thing is that with sites like these, you don't need to actually have a product for sale. You can just have an idea or a simple prototype, and then sites like these will allow you to test the market for your product by taking orders ahead of time. This way you can see if it will sell before you spend a lot of time and money on it. If you get a large number of pre-orders, you can then use that money to manufacture it.

Mobile Apps – If you have an idea for an app, you can have somebody on UpWork.com create it for you for as little as $200. I have created 20 iOS (iPhone/iPad) and Android apps, and they make around $600/month combined, but 95% of that income is from one app (Old Time Radio Shows for iOS). I put a lot of effort into creating the Dumb.com Old Time Radio Show Website over the years, so making the app was easy because it is just a simplified version of what was already on the site.

Offer A Service On Fiverr.com - For example, one of the musicians that creates songs for me on Fiverr.com told me he was working part time at a record store. He was making songs for me for only $25 each. I casually mentioned to him that he was too talented to be working at a record store and that he should do Fiverr full time. A week later, he quit his job and immediately had more Fiverr business than he could handle. He then raised his rate to $45 per song and is now turning away business because he is so busy. There must be something you are good at, so just do that. Draw things. Make funny videos. Review websites, songs, or books.

Start A Blog - Just go to a site like Wordpress.com or Blogger.com and within seconds you can be up and running with your own blog. You can use banner ads, such as those from Google AdSense), and you will start making money if you get any traffic. You don't need to know anything about web design or programming to start a blog, and to put the ads on your site, you basically just need to enter your AdSense account number.

Set Up An eBay Store – Thousands of people make a living selling things on eBay.com. Buy items at garage sales, municipal auctions, estate sales, and storage unit auctions, and then resell them online.

Real Estate Crowdfunding - Get in the investment real estate business. Sites such as RealtyMogul.com, RealtyShares.com, RealCrowd.com, and EarlyShares.com let investors buy shares in an investment property, kind of like how investors buy a stock on the stock market. The investor gets a percentage of the rental income from the property and a percentage of the profits once is sold. You can earn anywhere from 7%-18% or more on these investments. But, of course, there is risk, particularly if the real estate market crashes. Another way that you can make money from this is that you can find potential property deals yourself and then list them on these sites, allowing you to use other peoples' money to become a real estate tycoon.

Start A Website - You don't need to know anything about web design to start a site, and you don't need to spend any money at all. There are dozens of services that offer free websites, such as Weebly.com. They make their money by selling you extras, like domain names or shopping carts, but these are all things you can get later once you need them. Or, for around $5/month you can set up an account with a more traditional web host such as Hostgator.com or GoDaddy.com.

If you want to sell something, you should set up a merchant account so you can accept credit cards. You no longer have to do this through your bank. You can get a free merchant account almost instantly from sites such as Stripe.com or Paypal.com. Or, you can sign up for free to accept Bitcoin using a service such as CoinBase.com.

If your site is not e-commerce related, then you should put banner ads on it (like from Google AdSense), and you can instantly start making money. Keep in mind that if you start a blog or website that uses Google AdSense for your banner ads, be very careful to comply with their guidelines. Mainly, you can not have anything r-rated or inappropriate for kids. 95% of my ad income is from AdSense, and I constantly worry about my account being banned (this happens all the time to webmasters). If I lose my AdSense account, I will only make around 50% as much by running ads from another ad network. I recently had a site banned from AdSense because it was hacked, and I did not notice it, and the hackers wrote some obscene stuff on it. Another one of my sites was banned due to improper link promotion, although I am not sure why exactly. To reduce the risk of future problems like this, instead of running AdSense on all 300 of my sites, I now run it only on my top 20 sites. When I added it up, the 280 other sites were making less than $100/month from AdSense combined, so it is well worth it for me to give up that $100/month to lower my risk.

Sell Crafts Online - Do you like to make things by hand? Sell your goods on Etsy.com. Some example successes include purses, cat clothing, children's books, designer hair accessories, prints of paintings, and personalized cutting boards.

New Domains - There are thousands of new domain extensions (known as TLDs) that are becoming available as an alternative to .com, such as .money, .photos., .club, .reviews, and .ninja. Most of these new domains cost $10-$20 a year, although a few are hundreds or even thousands of dollars a year. It is very hard to predict how well each of these will do, but at least it is much easier to register them because not all the good ones are taken yet. For example, you could buy something like website.money or workfromhome.tips. You can then try to sell these in a few years once the new extensions become more popular. To see what domains are available, do a search at a domain registration site such as GoDaddy.com or Uniregistry.com. You can also look at recent sales prices of domain names at DNJournal.com, to give you an idea of how much you might be able to sell your own domains for.

Why I Bought A Flower Store

Since the time I started my own Internet company in 1995, almost everything I do is virtual. I work from home, don't go to meetings or go to trade shows, and hardly ever make phone calls. I have a paperless office, and my mailing address is a PO Box service that scans all my letters, allowing me to read them online. My voice mail box even tells people to email me instead of leaving a message (if they do leave a message, it is automatically converted to an MP3 file and emailed to me). So, it is kind of crazy that in 2002 I ended up buying a retail flower shop, even though I had never owned or worked in any type of store before and knew nothing about flowers. On top of that, I bought it online without ever seeing the store in person (it was 3,000 miles from where I lived). By the way, before I even closed on the buying the first flower store, I had a second one under agreement!

Here's what happened. For several years, I was using my GetFlowers.com domain name to sell flowers by earning a commission from another online florist for every customer I sent to their site. This made a little money for me, but there was no chance it was ever going to turn into a big flower site that way, so I decided to build my own online florist on it instead. I looked into it and figured out that most online florists were just order takers and sent out all their orders through floral networks such as FTD and Teleflora. These networks route the order to a local florist who delivers the flowers. All flower shops have a computer that runs FTD or Teleflora software, which they use to print the orders that are sent to them and also to enter orders from their customers for out of town deliveries. For example, if you walk into a florist in New York and ask them to send flowers to your grandmother in Miami, they will enter your order into their FTD or Teleflora system, and it is zapped to a florist in Miami.

The florists make a profit of around 20% for each order that they send through a floral network, plus they usually charge an extra fee (a "service charge") which they get to keep as a bonus. My plan for GetFlowers.com was to make it 100% automated and then to do away with any extra fees, as there was no work involved for me to place each order. I would set it up so that the customer just fills out the order form on my site, and their order is sent to the floral network who then relays it to the local florist. Most other floral websites at the time were not that automated, so when they took an order, they still had to manually re-enter it into the FTD or Teleflora system. Even if I got thousands of orders a day, the only work for me would be the customer service.

Another goal was to offer better customer service than other florists. Many florists are not well organized, and when they make mistakes, they are not willing to give refunds. They sometimes will redeliver the flowers for free if they mess up, but, for example, when it is five days after your mother's birthday that they missed, their offer does not help much. Another example is they sometimes will deliver the flowers, but forget to add the balloon you ordered. Or they will forget to add the gift card that says who the flowers were from. I think that if a florist loses your order and makes you look like a jerk for forgetting someone's birthday, just giving you a refund is not enough.

I decided to handle these situations differently than the other florists so as to always try to make the customer happy. For example, if Valentine's Day flowers were never delivered due to a mistake the local florist made, I would give the customer a full refund refund and pay out of my own pocket for the local florist to deliver an apology bouquet to the recipient. If it was just a partial screw up, then most of the time I ended up giving my customer at least double the discount the local florist gave me. Sometimes the local florist wouldn't give me any discount, but I still gave the customer a full refund.

Anyhow, to sell flowers at GetFlowers.com, I needed to be a member of the FTD or Teleflora networks. When I contacted them they told me it was a requirement that I own a real flower store, not just a website that took orders. So to start my GetFlowers.com website, I realized that I needed to buy a florist. Even though I knew nothing about running a flower store, I thought that maybe I could use my business and computer knowledge to make a struggling flower store more profitable. I would then buy more florists and make the operation into a big business. If eventually I had 100 flower shops, each making a few thousand dollars a month profit, I would be rich.

I checked out flower shops for sale on several of the leading business broker sites and found one listed for $40,000 in Huntington Beach, which was near my office in California (this was an office I had never been to because I ran it remotely). I had one of my employees (a web designer with no floral or retail experience) drive by and take a look. He liked the location, so I bought the store. As part of the sale, the previous owner agreed to work at the store full time and run it for me.

While I was working on buying the Huntington Beach florist, I happened to see a listing for a flower shop for sale in Sacramento for only $20,000, and the woman managing the store was interested in running it for me after the sale. There was no need at all for me to buy two florists, but it seemed like a good deal at the time, so I purchased this one also. I figured there would be some economies of scale in running 2 florists instead of 1, since certain costs (websites, marketing, payroll company, etc.) could be shared. Also, if I had only one florist and it failed, I might not know if the problems were related to that store in particular (like the location), and I still would have dreams of running a giant floral empire. But, if I had two florists that failed, at least I would get it out of my system once and for all and be done with it.

After I bought the florists, I was able to launch my GetFlowers.com website, although running the site really had nothing to do with the stores. I advertised GetFlowers.com in search engines, and it started getting several dozen orders a day. A few years later I bought the domain CheapFlowers.com (I think I paid $35,000 for it) and set it up as an alternate version of my GetFlowers.com website on it. I gave the CheapFlowers.com website a more wholesale look, with a long explanation about why I was able to offer such low prices. Although CheapFlowers.com was a catchier, more memorable domain, I was worried customers would be turned off by it because they might think it was a scam, or would worry about what to say if the person they sent flowers to asked where they bought the flowers ("Honey, I bought your flowers at CheapFlowers.com" does not sound so good). So, I made sure the credit card billing still showed the name "GetFlowers.com." Over time CheapFlowers.com has attracted more repeat customers, so that is the domain I have focused my efforts on.

Running the two retail stores turned out to be an adventure. Most florists run the store themselves and use the profits to pay their salary, but as an absentee owner, all the profits went to paying people to run the stores for me. That was fine with me, though, since my main goal was to make money from my flower websites and not the stores. The problem was that managing the stores was a lot of work for me, and there was little hope of making any significant money from them. I computerized both the stores, set up websites for them, did lots of online and off-line marketing, tried to get more wedding and corporate business, joined additional floral networks, created coupons, and even ran a flower kiosk in a mall, but none of that did much to help. The Sacramento store was in a mall that pretty much died after a few years, so sales dropped, and the store began to lose money. The Huntington Beach store did better, but still never did more than break even.

In some ways, owning the stores was easier than I expected. Rarely did something come up that I could not handle, and the existing employees in each store did a good job running things. But, just like with any business, there were constantly things that the owner (me) had to handle, like filling out paperwork, hiring and firing, advertising, bill paying, doing payroll, and dealing with suppliers, computer issues, insurance, sales tax, delivery van problems, etc. There also were frequent personnel issues I had to deal with, such as employees not liking each other, having personal problems, and accusing each other of things like stealing, lying, and drug use.

If the stores were making money, I could have hired somebody to handle all the "owner" stuff, but for me it was just a big hassle. I had hundreds of websites to run, in addition to doing all the mundane tasks of managing my company. My Internet projects had much more income potential than running real stores, so after a few years I shut the stores down. I was losing $5,000-$10,000 per month combined on them and could not afford to keep them open any longer. Luckily, I was doing a large volume of flower orders by then on my website, and FTD and

Teleflora by then were more accepting of Internet florists, so they did not care anymore if I had stores. Also, I hired the manager of one of my stores to do customer service for the website.

Like with any online store, the flower websites still have problems, such as fraud, server downtime, website errors, supplier issues, and more. But, it is much easier to run an online florist than it was to run the retail stores. Overall, I am still glad I bought the flower shops, because, without them, I would not have the online flower business that I have today. Although I did not become a retail flower tycoon like I had hoped, the important thing is that I gave it a try.

Domain Flipping

I consider myself a domain name expert, but even so I have not been able to make significant money with domain flipping. Much like with real estate, there is a big difference between an investor and a flipper. Investors buy domains and hold them for years, waiting for them to appreciate and waiting for the right offer to come in. Domain flippers buy a domain they think is undervalued, with the intent to sell it right away. Many times they need the cash to move on to the next deal.

One of my few successful domain flips was unintentional. In 2009, I bought the domain GameTheory.com for $6,901 at a Sedo.com domain auction. I purchased it because I thought it was cheap and would do well in Google if I built a site on it (Game Theory is the study of strategic decision making, as featured in the movie *A Beautiful Mind* about John Nash). A few days after I bought it, Sedo contacted me and said they had a buyer who read about the sale and would pay me $10,000 for the domain ($9,500 after the Sedo commission). So, I sold it for a quick profit.

Here are some other domains I bought in the past five years:

Pastries.com - $12,500
Adventure.com - $200,000
Humidifiers.com - $50,000
Physical.com - $42,500
Fairies.com - $32,500
AdvertisingAgency.com - $33,000
Feminism.com - $5,000
BrainTumors.com - $6,600

I did not have a particular plan for any of these domains, but I figured I would try developing them into sites. If that did not work out, I always could sell them for at least what I paid. I set up sites on all those domains, but none of them made any money at all. So, I decided to sell the domains. Some I sold for a profit, some for a loss, but for the big risk involved, and the large amount of money it tied up (that I could have invested in other opportunities), it was not worth it. I am happy though that I got to experiment with these domains, by both developing them and trying to flip them, so I don't regret any of it.

One of the best ways to buy and sell domains is through domain brokers. Many of them have frequent email newsletters they send out, listing all the domains they have for sale. It is worthwhile to sign up for their free newsletters just to get a general feel for domain pricing, even if you are not looking to buy right now. Here are some domain brokers you might want to look at:

MediaOptions.com
NameConnect.com
Sedo.com
Afternic.com
DomainHoldings.com
OutcomeBrokerage.com
DifferentInvestments.com
Brannans.com
Upmarketdns.com

If you are a domain speculator, keep in mind that now may not be a good time to invest in premium .com domains. I don't expect the domain market to crash, but there is a lot more risk then ever before due to all the new domain extensions (.coffee, .london, .rocks, .tech, etc.). When 866 and 877 toll free numbers first came out, it created a lot of confusion, and for the first time allowed almost any company to get a catchy toll free number when 1-800 previously was the only option. But for many years, people would call the 1-800 version of the phone number instead of the new 866/877 version, just like people often go to the .com domain by mistake even though the ad they saw was for a .net/.co/.biz site. Now many years later do younger people still get confused about the various types of toll-free numbers? I don't know, but just like with 800 numbers, adding all these new domain extensions creates an element of risk that did not exist before when .com was the undisputed king.

Other potential risks with domain investing include:

1. Internet users are switching away from websites (which use domains) and instead using mobile apps, Facebook apps, and Twitter hashtags, which means 5-10 years from now domains might have a lot less value. So far it has not made much of a difference in domain values because most companies still get a domain in addition to all these other types of media, but that could easily change over time.

2. The economy could collapse again like it did in 2008, and this might hurt domain sales. So far the Internet has kept growing so fast that domain prices have also kept rising, but that does not mean next time things could not get worse.

3. There is always the risk you might get sued over trademark issues. I have never had this happen, but it is fairly common. Many generic sounding domains may actually be covered by trademarks. Some recent UDRP complaints (this is the way domain disputes are arbitrated, outside of a courtroom) have been over domains such as:

Stages.com
Kite.com
GreatRun.com
HolidayRentals.com
Major.com
eBottle.com
Unbiased.com
PlayWorld.com
WorkBetter.com
SoapBoxDerby.com
FashionTV.com
Thesis.com

In many cases, the domain owner does not lose the domain, either because the domain is considered too generic, or because the domain owner has a legitimate right to it. But, just responding to a UDRP complaint can cost thousands of dollars in legal fees. More importantly if you lose, you will have spent a large amount of time and money building up your site and promoting it, only to have to give it up. To help prevent something like this from happening, you can do a free trademark search online at the United States Patent and Trademark Office. For example, if you want to buy the domain Blogs.com, don't just do a search for *Blogs.com,* also do a search for *Blogs* and also *Blog*.

Even doing a trademark search may not completely protect you. The way trademarks work, a company can have a trademark on a word or phrase even if they have not registered it with the Trademark Office. This makes it harder for them to win the case, but it probably will not stop them from filing it. The most important part of the trademark (either filed or not) is when they started using it. If they started using it before you bought the domain, you could be in trouble. In fact, if you bought the domain Blogs.com today and did a search and saw no trademark for the word *Blogs*, somebody could still register a trademark for it a few months from now or even years from now. As long as they prove they started using the trademarked word before you did, they would have a good chance of winning their case.

Here are two real life examples of domains I have owned that had trademark issues:

- Buffy.com - Back in 1997, attorneys for Warner Brothers sent me a letter demanding I give them the domain, because I was violating their trademark (from the movie and TV show *Buffy The Vampire Slayer*). They probably would not have been able to take the domain away from me, but if I set up a site about the show/movie, it would then be a trademark violation and they could take the domain away from me. As there was not much else I could use the domain for, I sold it to them for $1,000. I was actually happy with this outcome since that was my highest domain sale at the time.

- iPhonecalls.com - I still own this domain but have not developed it due to potential trademark problems. I registered it on August 23, 1999 (my intention was "i phone calls" as in "Internet phone calls"), and Apple did not come out with the iPhone until 2007. But, Apple obtained the trademark from Cisco, who obtained it in 2000 when it acquired Infogear, who registered the iPhone trademark in March 1996. So, even though I did not know it at the time I registered it, the term was trademarked. If I use the domain for a site that offers Internet phone calls, I may be safe, but I don't want to go up against Apple's team of lawyers.

The Story of DigiCredit.com

Back in the late 1990s, virtual currencies such as E-Gold and CyberCash were a hot trend, offering alternative payment systems for consumers to use on e-commerce sites. This appealed to people who did not have a credit card, and to people who at the time did not trust giving out their credit card info online. Years later, Paypal ended up winning the online payments battle, but before that (in 2002) I jumped on the bandwagon and started my own competing site: DigiCredit.com. It was a totally new type of payment service for websites that sold only digital goods (such as software downloads, eBooks, or memberships).

The way it worked was that people would make a purchase using the DigiCredit system and then pay for it later with real money. It was basically a promise to pay. No credit check, everyone was automatically approved to use it. All they had to do was fill out their name, address, and email address and promise to pay the bill within 30 days, and their order was instantly processed. The DigiCredit system would then email them a bill, and if they didn't pay after 15 days, it would keep emailing them reminders until they paid. They could pay the bill by mail using a check or money order.

On my DigiCredit.com site, I had a notice that said if they didn't pay, their account would get sent to a collection agency and be reported to the credit bureaus. But, I made that up just to scare people into paying. After a few years, to make it sound even more official, I added a section to the payment form where it asked the customer for the last 4 digits of their Social Security number for verification purposes. That part was fake too.

To launch DigiCredit, I added it as a payment option on FindCash.com (an old site I sold that is not active now), where users could see if they were owed unclaimed money by the government. It was free to do a search, but if their name was on the unclaimed money list, they had to pay $10 to find out how much they were owed and how to collect it. Because I was only selling data, my cost for each order was zero, so I had nothing to lose by trying DigiCredit as an alternative to accepting credit cards. The only potential problem with this test was that some of the people who paid by DigiCredit might have paid by credit card anyhow. But, as soon as I added the DigiCredit payment option to FindCash.com, overall sales increased significantly. That meant it was generating new sales.

None of that mattered though unless people were actually paying their DigiCredit bills. Because this had never been done before, I had no way of estimating what percentage of customers would pay. I could tell a bunch of the sales were fraudulent because fake names and email addresses were used, and I knew some customers would not pay their bill if they weren't happy with what they purchased. On the other hand, at least I no longer had to deal with credit card chargeback fees from these unhappy customers (chargeback fees were usually equal to 5%-10% of my sales, so it was significant).

In the end, approximately 20% of the DigiCredit customers paid their bills. Most paid within 30 days. Sending collections emails after that did resulted in few additional payments.

Even though 80% of DigiCredit customers did not pay, offering DigiCredit on my site still gave me a 10%-15% overall increase in my revenue, so I was happy with the results. I also saved paying the 2.5% credit card processing fees, although there was a little bit of work involved for me to process the payments (I had to mark each account as paid and sign each check and deposit it). I even used DigiCredit as a backup payment system for the times when my credit card processing was down (10 years ago things like that happened a lot more often), so that was basically free money. I normally would have lost all those sales.

I later used DigiCredit as the exclusive payment option on a few of my other small sites, because it was almost instant for me to set up, and I did not have to pay the monthly fees for a merchant account or go through the painful application process for one. I also started work on using it as an in-game currency on my Adoptme.com virtual pet site, where users could buy upgrades with it (like extra food or clothes for their pet). I also started building a premium section on Adoptme.com where people would pay a one-time $10 fee and then get lifetime access to special content. I was eager to do this because most of the users on the site were kids, so it would not have been effective to offer something like that using credit card payments. I envisioned giving kids a credit line at DigiCredit.com, and they could then spend this virtual money at participating sites (Adoptme.com would be one of those sites). Due to all the programming needed to add the upgrades system and the premium content section to Adoptme.com, I never got around to finishing this. I also received some interest from other sites who wanted to use DigiCredit, but I don't think the site owners would have liked the haphazard way I ran things (only collecting 1 out of 5 payments) so that never led anywhere.

All of this is similar in some ways to what Billmelater.com (now named "Paypal Credit") offers, but Bill Me Later is for adults only and does real credit verification using the last 4 digits of your Social Security number. They also charge you interest on what you owe. When Amazon.com started offering the Bill Me Later payment option, it soon became a hit, and the Bill Me Later company was bought by eBay for $945 million in 2008.

Eventually I ended up selling the Findcash website, so I shut down DigiCredit because it was not worth the trouble to run it just for the few small sites it was still being used on. I might do some more development of DigiCredit in the future, but for now I am working on building several Bitcoin-related websites instead, as I see a lot of opportunity in that industry.

Web Hosting Sucks

One of my biggest headaches over the years has been web hosting. Initially, I used shared web hosting (for small sites), but eventually my sites got big enough that I needed a dedicated server. Ever since, it has been one problem after another. I started with four remotely located dedicated Linux servers, but they were constantly crashing, so I kept buying additional remote servers (they cost $99/month each) to solve the problems. Eventually, I had 50 of them.

Managing 50 servers was a nightmare. Not a day would go by when there was not a technical problem on one of my servers or sites. Hackers, hard drive failures, bandwidth over usage, server errors, faulty equipment, memory overloads, etc. As web hosting technology improved, I eventually consolidated my sites to five servers, but those same types of problems continued. Over the years, I had tried several hosts that said they would manage my servers, like detecting when a server was down and fixing it, but most of them never did what they promised.

Tech support is always a big issue with any web host. My sites would sometimes be down for over 24 hours just because tech support was too incompetent to fix things. Then there are some hosts with great tech support, but their hardware or network constantly has problems. For several years I had my sites hosted with Colo4jax.com. I liked how they were able to customize my servers, and they offered great tech support. After two years of only small problems, their entire network was down for two days because they moved to a new data center and had some issues with the move. All my sites were down, and other customers were posting in a forum that Colo4jax might be out of business or that all the servers were lost. In the end, everything started working again, but it was a very stressful two days.

Another example of an annoyance with running servers is that Colo4jax.com once informed me that they immediately had to change the IP addresses on two of my five servers because their upstream provider was requiring this. This was a big pain in the neck for me because I manually had to edit several hundred DNS entries to make this change. To make matters worse, the next day my three other servers all stopped working. I realized right away that the problem was probably that these also needed new IP addresses, but of course Colo4jax.com never told me this. So then I had to spend another few hours manually editing several hundred more DNS entries, plus my servers were down for around eight hours.

When I sold Bored.com in 2008, the buyer told me he was talking with a web host that would do his hosting for $8,000/month and that $2,000/month of the price was for managing his sites/servers. I told him no matter how good it sounded, hosting would still be a huge headache for him. After a year, he still had the same types of problems I did, so he ended up canceling the management part of the hosting deal.

More recently, I have switched to cloud hosting, and that has solved many of the problems. It is much more reliable, and from a webmaster's perspective is not really any different to use it than any of my previous hosting accounts, so I didn't have to learn anything new. Two of the largest cloud hosts are RackSpace.com and Cartika.com. I use Cartika for my cloud hosting, although I also had a non-cloud server at Rackspace for many years and was very happy with them. The technical aspects of cloud hosting are different with each host, but the general idea is that instead of your site being on a single server that can easily go down or have other problems, it is in their "cloud" of servers which is much less likely to have problems. Seductive phrases such as "Fully redundant," "High availability," and "Self-healing" are used. Also, it is less expensive, because you only pay for the disk storage/RAM/CPU capacity that you need. As soon as you need more, it can be added on the fly.

All that is great, but no matter how reliable the hosting sounds, there can still be problems such as connectivity issues, server patching errors, and hardware failures. What is good about Cartika though is that when problems happen, they detect them and respond almost instantly on my behalf. I feel like they are always looking out for my best interests, and their tech support workers are acting as my workers. Plus, whenever I email Cartika sales or support, they respond quickly and go out of their way to give me the info I need.

Although the technical aspects of cloud hosting are impressive, many large website owners like me were using "failproof" type hosting a long time ago. As far back as the early 2000s, I used to use a load balancer with multiple servers to make it so there was little risk of downtime due to hardware failure. It was always pretty easy for me to add extra capacity whenever needed even without the cloud. I never once had the need to expand capacity faster than the day or two it took a host to manually do it. For various reasons, I still had lots of downtime (corrupt MySQL databases, DDoS attacks, load balancer problems, power outages, etc.). I had to keep an eye on the servers 24/7 because I had no faith at all that they would be running correctly. There was never a vacation I took when I didn't have a server crisis, or at least have to constantly check things to make sure there were no problems. What is different with my cloud hosting is that all the servers are fully managed, which means the web host automatically detects and fixes any errors/crashes for me. Also, because cloud hosting is set up much more efficiently than traditional hosting, it is usually much faster and easier for them to fix problems.

My advice to anyone looking for hosting is first to look on various web hosting review sites for info from existing customers about the web host you are considering. After you choose a host, you might want to hire a server monitoring and management company. They usually charge $25-$50/month to manage your server. Here are some to consider: We3Cares.com, AdminGeekZ.com, and PlatinumServerManagement.com. No matter what, you should use a free website monitoring service such as UptimeRobot.com, which will automatically notify you if your site goes down.

How I Invented A Plush Toy

In 2001, I created a virtual pet site at Adoptme.com, where kids could adopt free virtual pets (dogs, cats, horses, fish, etc.) and learn the responsibilities of pet ownership by feeding, walking, and taking care of their pets. It quickly became popular, with around 10,000 visitors per day and 2,000 new members per day. I had zero revenue from it though, because the site was designed in Flash and there was not really much space for ads on it. Plus, back then there were fewer choices when it came to putting ads on a site.

One idea I had to make money was to sell an AdoptMe plush toy (a stuffed animal with a soft, plush covering) in toy stores, where the plush toy looked just like the virtual pet the user adopted so they could play with the same pet both online and offline. The toy box had an ID code on it that the buyer could enter on the AdoptMe website to adopt the virtual version of the exact pet they bought. But, at the time I was overloaded just running websites and had no interest in doing any business that was non-virtual.

I happened to mention all of this to the person who set up my California office (the place I never went to), and he thought I was crazy for not trying to do more with AdoptMe.com. He offered to set up a partnership to handle the toy part of the business for me. As I had nothing to lose, because I was never going to do it myself, I agreed.

To make a long story short, it did not go too well. The good thing is that eventually we did get some plush toys manufactured (in China), and we started selling them at the AdoptMe.com website. I don't remember the exact figures, but our cost was around $2.00 per animal, and we sold them for $14.95. We sold around 1 a day, which was fine, but our goal was to get them in stores to sell millions and get rich. We got some sold in some small local stores and eventually, after much negotiation, we were able to convince Toys"R"Us to test the AdoptMe plush toys in their stores. Originally they were going to do a big test in 60 stores, but in the end they just placed an order for their Times Square NY store. This was one of their busiest stores, so it was a good place to test it at least. The AdoptMe toys ended up selling pretty well, considering we did no promotion other than advertising on the Adotpme.com website. But, in order for Toys"R"Us to continue selling a product in that high traffic Times Square store, it had to be a big hit, and our toy was not.

We could have tried to get the toy sold in other stores, but at this point three years had gone by and it was not making money. Product liability insurance alone for the toy cost $800/month, plus the costs of an employee and office suite. So, we decided to dissolve the toy company.

Several years later, Webkinz did the exact same thing we did, making hundreds of millions of dollars. Maybe we were just ahead of our time. I still own the AdoptMe.com website and it does well. Overall I am happy I was at least able to give the toy business a try, even though it did not end up making any money for me.

Working From Home

No matter how big my company gets, I will never work in an office. I love working from home. No commute, no dressing up, no meetings. I started my company 20 years ago in my apartment in Boston, but after a few years it got to the point where I needed an office. So, in 2000, I got one. I didn't work there though. I set it up 3,000 miles away in California. I figured even if I opened an office in the town where I lived, I would still never go to it. So when a business friend offered to set up an office for me in CA in an office suite on the same floor as his office, I took him up on it. He helped me hire a few employees to get it started, and he set up the furniture and computers. The fact that it was part of an office suite made it easier because they provided much of what I needed.

This worked out great for a few years, but soon everyone had high-speed Internet access and most things became web-based. As a result, I was able to have all those same employees work from home. I have never met any of them or spoken to them by phone, including some who have been working for me for over ten years. We just use email.

If you are looking to have work done for you, either hourly or by the project, here are a few sites you might want to try: UpWork.com (formerly known as oDesk.com), Freelancer.com, and Guru.com. Just do a search for the keyword you are looking for (*web design*, *Android apps*, *shopping carts*, etc.), and you will be presented with hundreds of workers, all listing the hourly rate they charge and what they specialize in. As an alternative, you can post a project to the site, and have workers bid on it. Often I will find the worker I am looking for and hire them, and they start working on my project that same day.

One of the issues when working from home is which mailing address to use. For some ventures, I would use a PO Box, but this becomes a problem if you move outside that area, so ten years ago I found an even better solution. Earthclassmail.com gives you a PO Box address and scans your mail so you can read it online. No more wasted time running to the Post Office every few days to get your mail. You can then choose to have each piece of mail forwarded to you or thrown out (or shredded and recycled). You even can choose to get a street address instead of a PO Box, which is handy for getting FedEx-type mail or for filling out forms that don't allow you to use a PO Box. All of this for $50/month.

I also used to pay $200 a month to my bank for a lockbox, but this is something Earth Class Mail can do instead. The lockbox was a special PO Box address I used just to receive checks. This was before the days of Paypal, Bitcoin, and electronic funds transfers. I would get over 100 checks a month (such as affiliate or invoice payments), and with the lockbox my bank automatically deposited the checks into my bank account on a daily basis, and then sent me a copy of each check for my records. Before I had a lockbox, I had to go to the bank several times a week to deposit checks (yes, I know, if having to go deposit money is my biggest problem in life, then I have it easy). Also, one time before I had the lockbox, I was out of town for three weeks and checks piled up in my mailbox, but I had no cash in my bank account. The unfortunate result was that I bounced some checks due to automated payments that were taken out while I was gone. Having a lockbox solves this problem. Because I already have a mailing address with Earth Class Mail, for an additional $35/month I can add their service where they deposit my checks electronically just like my lockbox used to do.

The Psychology of a Multi-Million Dollar Sale

In January 2008, I sold Bored.com and a network of 170 related sites for $4.5 million. This represented over half of my company and the vast majority of my profits. Bored.com was easy to run, had ten years of steady growth, and there was little risk that the income would go down. So, why did I sell?

The main reason I sold was so that all my wealth would not just be virtual. Having paper profits is great, but there is nothing like having lots of money in the bank. If the Internet keeps going up, I still have a big business that will keep going up in value. If everything crashes, at least I always will have enough money to live on.

That is the short version of the story, but there was really much more to it. Over the years, I had received some lowball offers for Bored.com, but never really considered selling because it made a huge amount of money ($35,000/month profit). But, I had spent the past 13 years working 7 days a week to build up my company, with the constant pressure of dealing with hundreds of emails and phone calls each day, and worrying about things like server crashes, payroll, accounting, potential lawsuits, bills, and taxes. I could not let anything slip through the cracks because it could have led to the downfall of Bored.com, so it was a lot of pressure.

In 2006, I got a multi-million dollar offer for Bored.com from a buyer (via a broker) who had bought some domains from me in the past. The problem was that he wanted me to finance much of the purchase price, and in addition he first needed to sell one of his big domains to raise the cash.

I had doubts if that would happen as easily as he thought it would, so I did not take his offer too seriously. Over the next year we went back and forth on various potential deals for Bored.com, and during that time I started to realize selling Bored.com might be a reality, even if I found another buyer for it. What at first seemed out of the question to me (life without Bored.com) suddenly became something I wanted to do. In fact, there was a period of a few months where I did not hear from the buyer, and I assumed the deal was dead, so I began looking for other potential buyers. I was now almost desperate to sell Bored.com, because I already had it in my head to do so. I dreamed about having all that money in the bank, working less, and focusing more on my family. In fact, at that point I didn't really care what part of my company I sold; I just wanted to cash out. One option was to keep Bored.com and sell my domain portfolio, but after I had solicited some offers, I realized the price would be too low to make it worthwhile. Plus, it took almost no work to run my domains, so it made more sense to sell what took up most of my time.

One reason I had not seriously thought of selling before was that my hope was to build Bored.com into a huge site, and then eventually sell it for a crazy inflated price like all the other Internet deals we all read about. If other similar sites could sell for $20 million, why couldn't mine? When the initial deal seemed dead, I shopped it around to companies like Google and Yahoo, but they all seemed to want larger, more developed sites. They wanted sites with members and with a more professional design. Bored.com was more of a fixer-upper type site for them, and they were not looking for that. I almost made a deal to sell it for $5 million to a small company that ran some sites similar to Bored.com, but that fell through because they buyer was having some business problems and needed to focus on other matters.

After several months of not having any interest in the site, a company I had previously contacted about buying my domain portfolio emailed me to say they might be interested just in Bored.com. Then that same week, my original buyer emailed me to say he was now ready to make a deal, and this time it would be all cash. At this point, I was willing to let go of the dream of selling for an insanely high price and settle for selling to whichever of my two potential buyers would pay the most.

My realistic goal was to sell for enough so I could put the money in the bank and live off the interest (bank CD rates were 5% at the time). I estimated that $5 million was an ideal amount, keeping in mind that I had to pay big taxes on this sale, and possibly a broker's commission (depending on which buyer I sold to). I also included 170 related sites in the package because Bored.com linked to or shared content with them, and they all linked back to Bored.com. Whoever ran Bored.com could manage these sites easily because they were set up similar to Bored.com. Also, if I did not sell these sites, the new buyer might decide to remove the links from Bored.com. If this happened, traffic to them would go way down and they would not be worth that much anymore. These supplementary sites added $5,000/month in net income, making the total net income around $40,000/month for the whole portfolio. Getting rid of this $40,000/month meant my company would have almost no ongoing profits, so that is why I had to make sure to have enough money in the bank to live on after selling.

The initial offer from each buyer was in the $3 million range, but by having them bid against each other over a two week period, I was able to get the new buyer up to $4 million and the original buyer up to $4.5 million. I had to pay a 10% broker's commission on the deal with the original buyer though, so that made both offers about the same. What eventually made me decide to go with my original buyer was that even though the new buyer was a much better fit for Bored.com, they wanted 6 weeks due diligence. That meant they needed one and a half more months to look everything over and they could back out for any reason during that time. The original buyer, knowing they might get outbid, offered to give me a $500,000 non-refundable deposit and the balance in 3 months, as long as I was willing to put the domains in escrow (to protect them from me running off with their $500,000) until the deal closed. If they backed out for some reason, I would get to keep their $500,000. This all sounded fair to me, so I took the deal.

The deposit part appealed to me because with big deals like this, many times things do go wrong, but this way at least I would have $500,000 no matter what happened. Plus, if I had $500,000 in the bank, I would not have cared nearly as much about selling Bored.com anymore, and maybe I would have kept the site. Putting Bored.com and the 170 sites into escrow was something I worried a lot about, because although I was getting a $500,000 deposit, there was still some risk. We chose Moniker.com to handle the escrow, but I worried what might happen if they went out of business during those three months, or if they got sued, or something else bad happened. I could potentially lose almost everything. Moniker.com assured me they had protection against that sort of thing, but there was nothing they could have said that would have made me feel 100% secure about it. Luckily, after the three months, the buyer paid as planned, and the deal closed.

The following are some other reasons I decided to sell:

1. Bored.com was a very Web 1.0 website. It did not have social networking, user uploaded videos, blogs, Facebook/Twitter integration, or any of the typical things that the more modern sites now have. It even had pretty much the same look and format it had ten years ago. I was always scared to change the site too much because Bored.com was such a big success, and I worried any big changes might cause the site not to be as popular. Also, I was 40 years old, and although I knew about all the latest Web 2.0 stuff, I was not really into it like most younger people were (I did not even have a Facebook account). Bored.com could probably have stayed the same for another five years, but eventually it would get too outdated. A new owner easily could do all these changes, and maybe make a lot more money from it.

2. I never did any direct ad sales for Bored.com; I just used banner ad networks such as Google AdSense and Casalemedia (now known as Index Exchange). A new owner could make double or triple the ad income by selling ads themselves, or redesigning the site to have higher paying ad formats. This made it more valuable to somebody else.

3. I constantly was having to think of new sites to create for Bored.com. After making over 200 of them, it became a lot harder to think of new ideas. I could have just stopped adding sites to Bored.com, but I worried what effect that would have on traffic.

4. There were some tax advantages for selling. I was able to structure the deal so I sold my entire company, instead of just selling my websites. This

allowed me to pay a lot less in taxes. If I had just sold Bored.com, it would have been treated like any other income, i.e., I would have had to pay up to 40% in state and federal taxes. By selling my company, it was considered a capital gain (like when you sell shares of stock in the stock market). Capital gains are taxed at much lower tax rates. Most buyers don't like deals to be set up this way because it makes it much harder for them to deduct the purchase price on their taxes. If they buy a website, they can deduct it, but if they buy a company they can't.

5. I felt like I had been in a casino for the past 10 years. Every day was a gamble, and I could lose it all at anytime. It was thrilling, but also exhausting. It was a nice feeling to walk away from the table with money in my pocket.

6. My entire company was run by me. If I ever died, it would be very hard for somebody else to take over. My servers would eventually shut down (from non-payment or computer problems that did not get fixed), and my sites would be almost worthless. Somebody could try to liquidate everything quickly, but it would be at fire-sale prices. Now if I die, my wealth will be more easily transferred to my family.

7. When I looked into selling in 2007, I was eager to try to close a deal quickly as I was pretty sure the economy was soon going to come crashing down, and I wanted to sell before that happened. I did not think my websites would get hurt much by a bad economy, but in a recession there are fewer companies spending big money to buy websites. I wanted to take advantage of the hot market while it lasted.

So, that was the end of this chapter of my life. Interestingly, not much has changed since then. I am still creating new sites, still buying and selling domains, still scheming on new ways to make money. I am glad I did the Bored.com deal, though, because it reduced my daily stress level and gave me much greater financial stability.

Publicity: Does It Bring Fame and Fortune?

A few years ago, I was interviewed about my domain name business, and although doing any interview is always exciting, what made this one different was that it was my first video interview. I had never used Skype (or any video chat type software) before, and I had only used a webcam a few times just to play around with it. It took me a few hours to get it all working correctly - USB conflicts (my keyboard and mouse stopped working when I hooked up the webcam), audio quality problems (I did not think the audio quality was good for the mic that was built into the webcam, so I tried 3 other microphones until I found one that was better), and trying to get the webcam positioned correctly (I put it on top of a stack of books in front of my monitor, but getting the height/distance/angle correct took some work). So, my only practice was a few minutes of Skyping with the interviewer (Michael Cyger) before the interview. Once I got the hang of it, though, it was fun.

My previous interviews were always by email or phone. Some were for newspapers, some were for business sites/blogs, and others were for radio stations. Most were about specific sites I owned. Either they wanted to feature my site because it was interesting, or they wanted my expert opinion about something relating to a story they were working on. I was quoted in the *Wall Street Journal* about backmasking (i.e., the hidden words you hear if you play certain songs backwards). I gave my opinion about the slang term "pimping" (as in "pimp my car") for a Florida Newspaper article about the controversy over a local church using that term in the title of one of their sermons,

Pimp My Life. I was on a panel of experts about fads. All of this was because I owned popular sites about these topics.

The funny thing is that I was not really an expert on any of these things. A typical Internet business owner has one site, and they spend all their time running it. They usually started the site because they have an interest in the topic. But, I have over 300 sites, the vast majority of which I am not an expert in, and don't even have a particular interest in. I just create sites I think will be popular (i.e., make money). I do learn a lot by running a site, so in many ways I am much more of an expert than the average person when it comes to things like Internet slang and playing songs backwards. But, I really am nowhere near the level of someone who has a passion for that kind of thing.

Another type of publicity I sometimes receive is when my sites get mentioned in the press. I have had sites featured in large media outlets such as *Entrepreneur Magazine*, *USA Today*, *Popular Science*, *The London Times*, *Inc. Magazine*, *Readers Digest*, *National Public Radio (NPR)*, and TV shows such as *Extra* and *TechTV*. What is interesting is that none of this publicity has ever resulted in significant extra traffic. Many times there is a good traffic spike for a few days, but then it all dies down after that. There is no lasting effect, and one media mention does not lead to many more, and nothing ever went viral.

I don't have a PR firm and make no effort to try to get publicity on my own, so these are just my personal experiences and may not be what happens with other Internet companies. Some businesses/products/sites get a little press and then ride the wave of publicity all the way to an appearance on Oprah, raking in the cash. I love getting press for my sites, and it certainly can't hurt, but I would rather grow my business by creating new sites instead of spending time trying to get publicity and hoping it will lead to something big.

My Human-Powered Search Engine

I have owned the domain name FindInfo.com for many years, and have tried creating various search engines on it. None of them have ever made any money. I know it is hard to compete with Google and Yahoo, but search engines are a billion dollar business and with a great domain like this I figured it was worth a try.

Back in the early 2000s, I made FindInfo.com into a site where you could win money by doing web searches. Each time you did a search, it would give you a point, and each point would give you an entry into the monthly cash prize contest. Users seemed to like this, but it never ended up bringing more traffic to the site. And, it was a hassle to deal with the programming bugs and giving out prizes each month.

Then in 2007, I decided to try making FindInfo.com into a human-powered search engine, where real people would help you find the search results you needed. ChaCha.com was already doing this, but they were constantly being criticized for the bad quality of their answers. This was because they used thousands of part-time workers spread throughout the world who were paid small amounts of money, and many of whom had limited experience and were unmotivated. I already was paying a company in India to do server support, and in the past they provided customer service for some of my sites, so I figured they could do a much better job at giving answers than the ChaCha.com workers.

In January 2008, I launched this new version of FindInfo.com, where users would first do a search the normal way (with the results powered by Google), but then if they did not find what they were looking for, they were given the option to have a FindInfo.com search consultant do the search for them for free via a live chat window. You can see some real examples of these searches, at findinfo.com/samples.htm. In addition to the live chat option, I also gave users the ability to call FindInfo.com by telephone to do a search for free. I did this by setting up a VOIP phone system and software in the same office in India where I had the workers. My total costs were $1,000/month for the workers plus $250/month for the VOIP system (which included the cost of phone calls from the USA to India).

After some technical glitches and a few weeks of practice, everything was running well. I added a link to FindInfo.com on Bored.com, and it was getting several hundred chat (search) sessions a day. The best thing was that as I had hoped, around 95% of the users just did the normal search, found what they were looking for, and never even used the human-powered search. That was good for me because I made no money from the human searches; I only made money from Google paying me as an affiliate for their searches. Another good thing was that I only got one or two phone calls (I made no money from those; I set that up just to make the site exciting and more legitimate looking). Also, initially I was worried about kids or troublemakers wasting my workers' time with "fake" chats, but that never was a big issue.

The problem was that the site never made a profit. It only made around $100/month in revenue from the Google searches, and more importantly, traffic to the site never grew over time. I expected people to love the fact that they could actually have real people help them for free, and although most users were happy with the answers they received, the site never built up a following and never got any publicity. By the end of 2008, I negotiated a new deal with the company in India to have fewer workers and lower the cost to $300/month, and I got rid of the call-in phone number. The site still kept losing money, though, so I closed it a few months later.

Is there a lesson to be learned from all of this? I am not sure. Maybe somebody else could have promoted the site better and had it take off. Or, maybe somebody else could have sold placement in the human-assisted searches (like if a user wanted a good online video game site, we would recommend a site that was good and also paid us). Maybe adding social networking features to the site would have helped, making it more of a community. I don't know what went wrong, but I still think it was a good idea.

Sharing

Ever try a neti pot? They are supposed to be great for preventing sinus problems. My mother gave me one many years ago, but I never used it. It sounded gross, and I was not sure I knew how to work it. But, I kept it just in case. Then one day, I was watching *Cougar Town* on TV, and the dad on the show used one. He was not at a doctor's office, and he was not magically cured; it was just a silly scene on a silly show. Suddenly I said to myself, "I can do that." So a few days later, I did. It was actually pretty easy and made me feel better. Sometimes you just need a little push (but not from your mother). This book is like that. I hope that by sharing my personal and business exploits, it will help people in their own lives. Often, it takes seeing someone else do something to nudge you to try it.

Some people like to share; other people like to stay private. When I was a younger, I hated changing my clothes in front of other kids. At camp I would rush to the locker room after swimming, so I would be done changing before the other kids even got there. Shirts and skins basketball games were a nightmare for me (when I was skins). Related to that, I went all four years in my high school without ever once using the bathroom, which was probably some kind of record.

Now in my 40s, I just don't care anymore. I'll answer the door in a towel if needed, and I don't check to make sure the shades are down when I get undressed. Maybe that is just part of getting older, but I assume that is also how the younger generation feels, with sharing photos of their lunch on Twitter, Instagramming selfies from a One Direction concert, and posting their relationship woes to Facebook.

It is about more than just releasing your inhibitions though. It is about wanting to share and wanting to be seen and heard. Before the rise of social networks, kids used to pass notes to each other in school. Some would also keep secret diaries and made a big deal about locking and hiding them. Just the act of writing it down was a form of sharing, even if nobody else read it.

Then came the Internet and everything changed. First, people started sharing in forums and chat rooms. Next was YouTube, where anybody could be a star. Soon, social networks led to oversharing. Now we are all part of the sharing economy. People share their apartments (Airbnb), their cars (Uber), and their money (peer-to-peer loans).

Unboxing videos. Ever heard of them? They show adults or children opening a new toy and trying it. It is kind of like a toy review, without the review part. With billion of views on YouTube, they are just as popular as the Justin Bieber and Frozen videos. You know another type of video kids are addicted to? Minecraft. Just watching people (mostly adults, such as Stampy) play Minecraft, talk about it, give hints and tutorials, and act silly. No wild stunts, no explosions, no crazy cats or epic fails. Just simple sharing.

I write books to be heard. I write songs to be heard. When I make websites, I get satisfaction from knowing people use something I created. And, each website is in some way an expression of myself. With each new book, song, or website, I feel like I am giving birth (yes women, I know it is not really the same). I labor over it, have high hopes for it, and then set it free into the world. Fly little book/song/website, fly.

Are Website Makeovers Worth It?

Many people will probably disagree with what I am about to say, but I think too much value is placed on giving a website a makeover. Obviously it is always good to improve a site, but I'm told all the time that if I do this or that to my sites, the site will make a lot more money. My own experience has been this is not usually true. Sites like Facebook.com and Amazon.com would never have blown up like they did, had they not spent a huge amount of time improving their programming and graphics, but on the other hand Google became a big hit just by having a very simple looking site that has had very few changes over the years.

I am sure there are many webmasters who can tell you tales of how they improved their sites, and it made a huge difference for them, but here are some of my stories:

- Adoptme.com - I created this virtual pet site in 2001 and by 2007 nothing much had changed. It was getting several thousand visitors a day, and I was making around $3,000/month from the ads on the site. Over the years, traffic never increased, and I think after a few weeks users would get bored with it. I had not done updates for several years, and it was a very Web 1.0 type site. I had the idea that maybe if I made it like a Facebook for virtual pets, with social networking and all the usual Web 2.0 features, it would be a much bigger hit. If I could get ten times as many visitors, or even just have the existing visitors go to the site ten times as often, then it would make $30,000/month instead of $3,000/month. In 2008, I added cool features kids would like such as blogs and profile pages for their pets, pet groups, the ability to private message other pets, jobs for pets, greeting cards for pets, pet music videos, fashion accessories to dress up their pets, pet of the month contest, an Adoptme Facebook app, pet jigsaw puzzles, and pet video games. To top it off, I then added something no other virtual pet site had. It was a mind-blowing breakthrough in technology that I thought would rock the virtual pet world. I gave Adoptme.com users the ability to chat live with their virtual pets. Not just some random dog or cat or horse, but they could now chat with the actual virtual pet that they had adopted. It knew its own name; it knew the owner's name; it knew when its owner last fed it. It was like talking with a real animal (if animals could talk). I got many emails from kids asking me if these pets really were chatting with them, and parents emailed me to make sure it really was a computer and not a real person (pretending to be a pet). I sat and waited for the million buyout offers to come in (MTV bought Webkinz.com for around $160 million and Disney bought ClubPenguin.com for around $700 million), but the phone never rang. I even issued a press release and made some posts on virtual pet forums, but nothing happened. I am sure kids who visit the site like it a lot more now, but 7 years have passed and traffic has declined every year.

- In the 1990s and early 2000s, I owned an online vitamin store named GetVitamins.com, where I sold vitamins at discount prices. When I started the site, it was basically just a text only list of vitamin names and their prices, along with a simple shopping cart. Over the years I added photos of the vitamins, product descriptions, and a nice looking site design. But, from what I could tell, none of that increased the conversion rate from the ads I placed, or caused any increase in sales. You have to keep in mind that my goal was to offer the lowest prices for vitamins, so having a cheap warehouse-type look went well with that theme.

- Dumb.com - For many years I kept dumb.com (funny videos, silly jokes, crazy photos, etc.) looking like a very simple site from the 1990s. In 2008, I decided to give it a Web 2.0 makeover, but that did not bring any extra traffic to it. I also added a user registration system to the site, allowing people to create profiles and make comments about the content. That was a total flop. In 2015, I had it redesigned again (and got rid of the user registration), partially so it would be "responsive" (meaning it would look good on mobile devices), and just to look more modern. Again, this had zero effect on traffic and income.

- When I started Bored.com in 1997, it was just a simple list of text links to fun and interesting sites. Over the years, it grew into such a popular site, so that I always was very hesitant to change anything, for fear traffic might go down. Maybe the odd look of the site made people remember it better and stand out from the crowd, or maybe people liked how it loaded fast (hardly any graphics to slow it down) and was easy to navigate. Or, maybe people hated the look and feel, but the search engines liked it, and that was really what mattered. By changing the format, I could easily have lost a huge amount of traffic from the search engines. After 5 or 6 years, I finally gave the site a graphical makeover to make it at least look presentable, but I still got complaints it looked very old. Everyone suggested I add more modern social networking (Web 2.0) type features. After I sold Bored.com in January 2008, the new owner experimented with several new formats (including a blog type format). He greatly reduced the number of links on the main page and completely deleted some of the category pages. He also changed the focus of the site to be more on video games, and then later to viral videos, and more recently to viral articles. I used to be obsessive about making sure all the links worked and fixing any site errors right away, but for a few months while the new owner moved servers, I noticed around 20% of the links and pages on Bored.com were not working correctly. In the end though, it seemed none of the format changes or error problems caused any significant change in traffic or income.

What is my point from all of this? I am just saying you shouldn't have too high expectations from improving your site. It won't always get you more traffic or more income, and sometimes will just be a waste of time and money.

Taking Your Business To The Next Level

One of the biggest problems in running an Internet business is taking it to the next level. By that I mean that many sites eventually get to the point where they make money, but profits and sales level off, and the owner can't figure out what to do to get rich from the site.

As an example, I currently have this problem with CheapFlowers.com. Although I get several hundred orders a month, I am just breaking even. Yes, I can advertise to get more sales, but all the ads I have ever placed lose money. What drives me crazy is the way I have the site set up, it could easily handle 500 orders a day (or even 5000). Almost everything is automated, so it would involve no extra work, and I would not incur additional expenses. Those extra orders would be pure profit (I make around $10 per order).

I used to have the same problem when I ran my GetVitamins.com website. Vitamins are a huge business online, so you would think a site would have a lot of growth potential, but I could never get past the 10-20 order a day level. I tried adding a lot more products, but that did not help. I tried adding more product photos, but that made no difference. I made changes to the shopping cart and the text on the site, but nothing changed. I was making $2,000/month profit from the site before I closed it, but running it was a lot of work. I was doing all the customer service myself, and that was taking up a great deal of my time. There were also constant inventory, shipping, and website problems. As it did not seem to have the potential to grow, after five years I decided to close it and move on to other business ventures.

I am involved in partnerships with FindRentals.com and BargainPrinting.com, where other people do all the marketing and promotion and advertising, and both these sites have that same growth problem. It took many years to get them to the level they are at now, but the real profits would come pouring in if sales were to double or triple. Just like with my sites, these sites are all set up to handle a lot more business, but they just can't figure out what to do to obtain it.

I am not sure what the answer to all this is. I have not found any way to boost traffic significantly to my most important sites (such as Dumb.com and Adoptme.com), or any way to get more orders for CheapFlowers.com. I have tried press releases, viral videos, link trades, search engine optimization, online advertising, offline advertising, adding unique content, and anything else I can think of.

The main two areas I had big success in online were both situations where the industries went to the next level, and I went along for the ride. I bought domain names in the 1990s, and they made almost no money back then. But, in the 2000s the domain market exploded, so my portfolio of domains suddenly became a big business. Bored.com took the leap from being a small site to a big success partially due to the huge growth of the Internet since 1997 when I started the site. This led to the number of visitors to increasing substantially each year. Also, in the early 2000s, the online ad market took off, causing ad rates on Bored.com to skyrocket. In addition to having many more visitors, I was making more money from these visitors. Both of these factors were a much bigger influence on the success of the site than all the various things I did to promote Bored.com or add great content to it. Of course, there are lots of sites that do all these same things and do take things to the next level, so maybe I am just not good at that aspect of my business, or maybe a lot of it is luck.

Another solution is not to worry about that problem, and instead focus on creating or buying new websites. For example, years ago my mother started a clothing directory website. She put a huge amount of work into creating the content, and I helped with the technical end. Soon after its launch, she created a related directory, and the sites were making a profit of around $300/month combined. This was much higher than I expected, but it is still is not a lot considering the many hours each month she spent on it. Despite various changes she has made to the two sites over the years, income has gone down. Realistically, I don't think there is anything she can do to take it to the next level. But, somebody with more time, energy, and ambition might look at her directories as a successful starting point, and decide that if they built 20 such directories, they would then be making $3,000/month instead of only $300/month. Once you are running 2 directories, it might not be that much harder to run 20 of them. My mother would say this would be impossible for her, as she barely has enough time to run the ones she has now, and that the quality of their content would have to suffer drastically. I would argue that after her initial work to create the 2 sites, they might make just as much money if she did the bare minimum amount of work. In my experience, I have not always found that putting a lot of work into maintaining and improving a site leads to making more money from the site.

She could instead focus on creating 18 more sites, and then pay somebody else to run them for her. For $250/month, a team of programmers and customer service reps overseas would be happy to handle everything. I know this because I have had them do the same thing for some of my sites. She initially would cut her income in half (from $300/month to $50/month after the site management fee), but she would have the potential to have the income increase to $3,000/month (actually it would be $2,750/month after the management fee).

I tried a similar plan in the early 2000s with e-commerce sites. I was making $2,000/month from GetVitamins.com, which was good, but not enough to make that big a difference in my company overall. So, I decided to open 15-20 new online stores (candy, cookies, fish, jewelry, caviar, and more). With all these sites, including GetVitamins.com, the products were drop shipped to the customer (my supplier mailed them directly). This way I didn't have to deal with a warehouse or inventory. I did have to handle all the customer service, all the suppliers, all the messed up shipments, all the website errors, all the different credit card merchant accounts, all the fraudulent orders, and more. Each of the sites made a small profit ($100-$1,000/month), and I could have opened more, but at that time I was doing everything myself and was busy enough. After a year or two, I began looking at these extra sites as a burden and eventually shut them down. I should have just hired somebody to run them for me. Even so, I would have had to spend a significant amount of time on them, and that would have left me less time to focus on my domain names and Bored.com, which were the main parts of my business.

In the mid-2000s, I tried this type of plan again by buying approximately 100 non-e-commerce sites over a two-year period, but none of them ever made much money. Each deal involved a lot of time and effort on my end: negotiating with the seller, taking the site over, moving it to my server, changing the ads to my own accounts, fixing problems on the site, taking over support for the site, and dozens of other small tasks. This was not something I easily could delegate to somebody in India, and I did not have anybody who worked for me directly who knew how to do that kind of stuff. Once each site settled into my network, it was not a huge amount of work to run them, but I also never made enough to make it worth the initial cost and the work involved. If my company had been set up ahead of time so I could have had somebody handle most of this for me, then maybe things would have gone a lot better. Yes, it all added to my income, but had I focused my efforts on other things, I may have made a lot more money. Or, maybe I should have just bought one big website instead of 100 small ones.

In the end, I am still glad I tried starting the online stores and buying all those sites. Had other areas of my business not done so well, I could have focused on these sites instead. And, I learned a lot from doing it. I think the lesson to take away from all of this is that you should not feel stuck if you have a website that won't grow any bigger. There are always other related things you can do to make more money, even if this deviates from your original plan.

My First Date

Sometimes business is a little like dating. Let me explain. I went on my first date when I was in 7th grade. It was typical middle school stuff. I had a crush on a girl in my class (I will call her "Amy") and was flirting with her, so she had her best friend ask me if I liked her. I said "Yes." A few days later, Amy casually asked me what I like to do on weekends. I told her I usually go to the Fun & Games arcade on Saturday mornings. She said she sometimes goes there too. I said, "Great, maybe I'll see you there."

I was not sure if this was now an official date or just idle chatter, but since I really did go to this arcade most weekends, I figured I would go as usual and hope she showed up. I woke up that Saturday morning and realized it was a gigantic snow storm. Hardly any cars were on the road, and I worried the arcade might be closed. I told my parents I wanted to ride my bike there, and they thought I was crazy. (I did not tell them about the "date" because I was not sure it even was one.) After some nagging, they gave in and let me go.

Just as I got to the arcade, I saw Amy riding up on her bike. I was overjoyed. We walked in together, but then I had no idea what to do. I was not sure if I should play video games with her, or if we should do our own thing and just meet up every now and then. It was awkward, but in a sweet way. We played some together, some apart, but felt connected just being there. After an hour or so, her dad came to pick her up (so she wouldn't have to ride her bike home in the snow), and by then it felt like a real date.

We ended up going out for a year and a half and were madly in love. We were voted best couple in our school. We wrote dozens of long notes to each other, we held hands on romantic walks, and talked (via notes) about having our first kiss (she was nervous about it, so it never really happened). Then she broke up with me over the summer. I am not sure why; she may have met somebody else. She ended it over the phone (there was no texting or emailing back then), even though we had promised if we ever broke up, we would do it in person. We also had said if we ever broke up we should meet when we were 30 and catch up. That never happened either. But, those 18 months were some of the most exciting and intense times of my life.

My first few years of running my own business were kind of like this. Everything was new, every day was filled with adventure. A whole new world was opening up to me. I didn't really know what I was doing, I just learned as I went along. Sometimes I lost, sometimes I won. One door would close, another would open. After around ten years in the Internet business, I felt like I had pretty much seen it all and done everything. This was not a bad thing, just different. Kind of like how some people feel being married after ten years. Good and comfortable, but lacking the thrill of your wild and crazy days.

Some people are happy with life; others have a mid-life crisis, change everything, and start over. The good thing about the business world, at least on the Web, is that it is never too late to change direction. "Pivoting" a business is now considered trendy. Expanding by buying other businesses is looked at as a healthy way to grow. Starting multiple companies is considered smart and entrepreneurial (think Richard Branson, Elon Musk, Mark Cuban, and Donald Trump). Much like the dating world, the Internet is filled with endless opportunities. You just need to put yourself out there to take advantage of them.

Domain Development

At one point, I had over 9,000 undeveloped domain names. In the 1990s, I had many of them set up on a system that I created where I manually put affiliate links on them, targeted to the topic of each domain. Maintaining these sites was a lot of work because affiliate programs were always changing, so I would have to constantly add/edit/delete the links.

In the mid-2000s, domain parking companies started offering a service where they set up domain pages for you, and gave you a percentage of the income from the ads and paid links on the pages. This worked great because there was almost no work involved on my end. For a few years, I was making around $10,000/month more revenue from domain parking than the $6,000/month in monthly domain expenses (renewal fees) that I was paying. Then in the late 2000s, domain parking income decreased so much that I was not making enough to cover the costs. I made up for the lost monthly income by selling a few domains per month, but that was not a good long-term business plan.

Also, parked domains do badly in the search engines (as they are really fake pages nobody would ever want to go to). Over the years, Google has improved their algorithms to detect them and not send them any traffic. Currently, I estimate that 90% of my parked domains don't even make enough money to cover the annual domain registration fee (I pay $9/year per .com domain).

To move away from parking, five years ago I tried an experiment where I built what are known as mini-sites on 4,000 of the domains that were making no money (so I had nothing to lose). A mini-site is a simple website created around the topic of the domain name, for the purpose of getting listed in the search engines. I created a mostly automated system to generate these pages that allowed me to choose a keyword for each domain (e.g., GetMortgages.com would use the keyword *mortgages*). I filled these pages with relevant articles (approximately 14,000), news stories, and videos. After a year, I was just making enough from these domains to cover the cost of the server ($80/month). It was not worth the effort, and I changed them all back to being parked (I use DomainNameSales.com). I probably should have just kept the server running, to see if the income would improve over the years, but I didn't. From many articles I have read about mini-sites, I am pretty sure I made the correct decision.

I have heard that some domain owners make a lot of money by taking one big domain, putting lots of content on it, and optimizing it to get listed well in the search engines. A few years ago, I decided to try this with three domains: Ailments.com, iAnimals.com, and WaterTowers.com. For Ailments.com, I paid a company in India to write articles about thousands of medical conditions and diseases. iAnimals.com started off as a site with around 4,000 animal photos, which I bought for $5,000 and added animal videos, jokes, games, and other animal-related content. WaterTowers.com was a domain I bought for $2,000 in December 2007 right after watching a segment on the Today Show about water towers. I had never thought about them before and knew nothing about the topic, so I figured a website about them might interest people.

Some of these sites got good search engine listings, but none of them made money. At best, I made $10/month from 1,000 visitors a month to each site. Even ahead of time, I knew none of these sites had the potential to become huge hits, so I decided to try something bigger. I changed my WatchMovies.com domain from being parked to having actual content on it (with banner ads). It instantly started making 50% more money. This was partially due to the domain parking company taking a big cut of the earnings. Once I stopped using them, I was getting 100% of the revenue.

My main motive for developing WatchMovies.com was to get it listed in the search engines, so it received more traffic. When the domain was parked, it had almost no traffic from the search engines. Because movies are extremely popular online, the phrase *watch movies* received a significant number of searches. Even if a small percentage of those searchers went to WatchMovies.com, it would have been a huge windfall for me. I made a simple one page site, and traffic did end up going up as I predicted. When I added even more content (500 public domain movies people could watch online for free and movie reviews and trailers), however, it had almost no effect.

I also created 200 of what I called "super mini-sites" when it was clear that my regular mini-sites were not working out. I changed 200 of my best mini-site domains to use Wordpress (a web page creation program) instead, with a custom template design for each site, and much higher quality articles for content. Unfortunately, these sites did not do any better than the previous mini-sites.

Next I took some old sites that were not making any money, and changed them all to use Google Custom Search. This is a service that lets me offer a mini Google search engine on my page, using their results, but it only searches a specific topic. Like for my FindHosts.com site, it just shows web hosting related search results. These search results show the same ads Google does, so I make money when a user clicks on the ads. Here are some of the other search sites I created:

SuperPhotos.com - A photo search engine
FindBlogs.com - A blog search engine
KidV.com – Kid videos
FindInfo.com - A Google-type search engine
FindFlorists.com – A florist search engine

None of these sites are making any money either.

One thing I should clarify is that I don't advertise or promote any of my sites. If you are looking to develop a site where you are going to invest money on marketing, then having a great domain should give you a significant advantage. My results are strictly search engine related.

People are always telling me another way to get additional traffic is to add more content to my existing sites. You would think this is sound, logical advice, but in my 20-year history of running over 400 sites, I have not found this to be true. My results may not be typical, and I am sure lots of people make good money by having thousands of pages on their sites and keeping them constantly updated, but not me. Here are some of my observations about this topic:

1. I have just as many one or two-page sites that rank at the top of Google search results as I do big sites with lots of pages that rank well. Many small sites that I created in a day do just as well as huge content sites that I spent months working on.

2. Aside from the quantity of the content, I also have found that the complexity of the site does not matter much. Over the years I have created many simple sites (silly lists, joke pages, online quizzes etc.) and also created many complex sites (online

stores, neural networks, large databases, etc.), and have not found much of a difference in the profits. Sites that cost me $1,000 to create have earned $0, and sites that cost me $0 to create have made $1,000.

3. Once I launch a site, I have not found adding more content usually adds any significant traffic or income to it. If you launch a bad site that is lacking in content, it should be improved later. At whatever time I decide a site is complete, however, I have not found adding to it helps any. For example, I paid one Flash designer over $50,000 for various animation projects over the years, all of which were funny, well done, and great content to add to my sites. Yet, none of it made more than a few hundred dollars in extra revenue.

4. For many years, I had a graphics designer working for me full time, and the sites he created looked amazing. I also created many sites myself that had no graphics at all (I don't know how to do graphics), and most of those sites did just as well. I have had the same results with site redesigns. When I first started Bored.com in 1997, it was just a plain text site with a list of links on it. I hardly changed the look of the site for the first five years. Eventually, I added some graphics to it, but even then everybody said it looked like an amateur, outdated site. Before I sold it, I did a few more fancy site designs, but none of that ever increased the traffic or ad revenue.

5. I have found the main advantage of changing a site design is optimizing ad sizes and placement. Where you put the ads, and which ad format you choose, sometimes make a big difference in how much mon-

ey you make. As an example, I recently doubled the income on one of my sites in five minutes just by moving a 728x90 AdSense banner ad from the bottom of the page to the top of the page. Many times, changes like that can be done without really changing the main site design; it is just a matter of rearranging things slightly on the site.

I am not telling people to avoid adding content to their sites or making them look nice. And, no matter what there is a significant benefit in that it feels better to own a great looking site. What I am saying is that in my experience, the cost of doing these things is usually not worth it. I would rather add a text page of content (like putting a list of jokes on my site at Dumb.com) for free instead of paying to add expensive programming/content. Adding more content is hardly ever a bad thing; it is just a matter of making sure it will make more money than you spend on it.

After I was fed up with building mini-sites on my domains, I decided to set up a bunch of more ambitious, complex sites in the hopes that those would do better. So far none of them have made any money either. Here are some examples:

- PickStocks.com – Initially, I set it up to rank stocks based on their social media popularity, to try to predict which stocks will go up and down. I also had somebody write custom profiles for 500 of the largest stocks, to help the site get good search engine listings. The site ended up only getting 2-3 visitors a day. I then changed it to have extremely sophisticated programming that allows people to backtest their stock picking strategies, to try develop systems that will beat the stock market. Still no traffic.

- LocalRecap.com - Local info for each city and state in the USA. I paid for custom written content for the 50 states and several hundred cities. The site gets less than 5 visitors a day.

- BigCelebrities.com - Social media rankings for over 15,000 celebrities using a proprietary formula that I created. I also had profiles custom written for 5,000 of the most popular celebrities. Kind of like Klout.com, but more entertaining. I even added a page where people could upload their photo ,and it would show them other Facebook users who looked like them. The site gets less than 50 visitors a day.

- CoverFights.com - Vote for which cover song you like best. I found and watched hundreds of videos on YouTube and added each one manually to the site. Gets less than 10 visitors a day.

- BigFansites.com - A large directory of celebrity fan sites. No traffic.

- FindClichés.com - A list of hundreds of popular clichés and their meanings. No significant traffic.

I did set up a few sites that bring in decent income, such as:

NurseryRhymes.com - I paid $13,050 for the domain in 2011 and once I set up a site on it (a list of over 1,000 nursery rhymes and their lyrics), it got listed at the top of Google and made anywhere from $300-$1,000/month. I sold the domain/site in 2015 (I can't disclose the price).

Metaphors.com - I paid $2,500 for the domain in 2012, and soon after set up a site listing common metaphors and their meanings. It makes $50/month.

I am happy with these outcomes, but they were not get-rich-quick type investments. More importantly, for every domain that did well, I purchased two or three other domains that made no money at all after I developed them. After taking the losing domains (OfficeHumor.com, DumbVideos.com, etc.) into account, I did not make any profit.

Next, I set up a bunch of online arcade sites on 20 video game domains. I used software from wparcade.com with a selection of over 2,500 games. The sites got no traffic.

I then decided to try creating Wordpress article type sites again, but this time on my most valuable domains, such as Weights.com, Pastries.com, Hoaxes.com, Physical.com, TattooShops.com, and AdvertisingAgency.com. I made sure the sites had great designs and very high-quality articles, all targeted at high traffic keywords. Still no significant traffic (5-10 visitors a day per site on average).

I also set up some simple one-page sites with good, unique content that I compiled myself. Some examples include GreatProverbs.com, DumbInsults.com, CelebSayings.com, and OfficeSlang.com. Again, hardly any traffic.

I know I shouldn't just create new sites, and automatically expect them to do well. I tried social media marketing (promoting sites on Facebook, Twitter, etc.), but found it did not make much of a difference. Any spikes in traffic it caused soon faded away. One way that I know it did not help is that on some of my sites I use a WordPress plugin to automatically post a link on Facebook and Twitter to all of the new content. Sometimes this plugin stops working for weeks or even months, yet I have never seen any decrease in traffic to those sites during those times.

How My Web Host Screwed Me Out of $5,000

A few years ago, I had a dispute with one of my web hosts, so I thought I would share it with you, as an example of one of the challenges of running a company. For many years, I had most of my sites hosted at Colo4Jax.com, which is a small web hosting company that offers very low prices and personalized service. In the last few years I hosted with them, they had a large amount of downtime. Once, all my sites were down for over two days, another time they were down for 14 hours, other times for a few hours. Although this was not good, I have always had bad experiences with web hosts, so none of this was horrible enough to make me want to go through the huge trouble of switching hosts.

Then cloud hosting started getting popular, so I decided I would give it a try. I moved some of my sites to Cartika.com. Although it was not perfect, it was much much better than any other hosting I had ever used. It took me almost another year to move all of 300+ my sites. Over that year, I canceled my Colo4jax servers one by one as I was done using them, and in the process I happened to discover that Colo4jax.com was double billing me for one of the servers. I am sure it was an honest mistake on their part, but the end result was they overbilled me by $5,555 (this is the amount they calculated in an apology email to me after I emailed them about it).

Before I continue with that story, let me first tell you about another billing problem I had with them. A few years earlier, I prepaid them $743 to set up a backup server and internal network, so I easily could make backups of all my sites. Unlike the normal servers they set up, this involved some custom configuration to create a private network for my servers so the data could be backed up much faster. It was the kind of thing web hosts do all the time, but not something they could do for me instantly. It should have only taken a week at most, but after one and a half years and several emails to them about why they never set it up, I gave up and canceled the order and asked for a refund. Despite many promises of sending me a check, they never did. Finally after several more months (and many nagging emails from me), they sent me $600 and promised the other $143 in a few days. But, they never sent it (despite many more emails from me).

When I discovered the $5,555 double billing error, it was a year after I demanded a refund for the backup server that they never set up, and for which they never fully refunded me. Due to the problems with the previous refund, I knew there was no hope they would ever refund the $5,555 they overbilled me, even though they did not dispute that they owed me the money. So, when they offered to give me hosting credit for the $5,555, I accepted, because I had no other choice. Normally, I would not have cared about getting a credit vs. a refund, but since I was in the process of shutting down all my Colo4jax servers, it was not what I wanted. But, I figured I would just keep a few of my sites hosted with them long enough to use up the credit.

In the subsequent months, however, there were even more downtime problems with Colo4jax, so I decided to switch all my sites to Cartika and shut down my all my Colo4jax servers, even though I still had over $2,500 in credit with them. The problem was that when I asked them for a cash refund of the balance of the credit, they said no because I already had agreed to take it as a credit.

I am not sure of the exact legal issues involved, but I would think that overbilling a customer and not refunding it would be considered fraud, as it basically amounts to stealing money from me. Once they found out about the billing problem and refused to refund it, it was no longer just an honest mistake on their part. And, to make matters worse, they did it twice, since they had done it once before by charging me money for the backup server that they never set up, and then never fully refunded that money (despite all their promises to do so).

Seller's Remorse

In February 2014, I bought the domain GameReviews.com for $7,000 (Estibot.com values it at $63,000). Over and over again I had vowed to stop buying domains, because I was not making money from them, but I saw this domain for sale in an email newsletter and felt compelled to buy it. I did not have any particular plans for it and am not that into video games; I just thought it was a good deal.

I figured I would try to set up a game review site, and if that did not work, I could always sell the domain for what I paid for it. I did not want to pay to have people write game reviews since there are already hundreds of sites that do that, so I decided to set up a big site of existing reviews. I bought review site software for $250 from Crowdvox.com, but also purchased a video game review script from GameSpotClone.com for $197 and then imported their review database (6,500 reviews, 13,000 videos, 196,000 images) into Crowdvox.com. I did not want to use just GameSpotClone.com because I figured there were too many other sites already using it so Google would not consider the content unique, plus Crowdvox.com had some features that I liked.

I got a working version of the site up and running, but it never got any traffic from Google. Because I was experimenting with selling domains on Flippa.com at the time, I decided to post the site for sale. The highest bid was $9,000, and my reserve was $20,000, so it did not sell. I had a private offer by email for $12,000, and another buyer said they could probably pay more than that, but needed time to come up with the money. Another buyer wanted to pay $25,000 but finance with payments of $1,000/month.

Just about the time I was getting all these offers, I had an idea for a new version of the site and really wanted to give it a try. But, I knew there was a good chance it was going to make $0 just like most of the other sites I have launched in recent years, so I was not sure what to do. I could double my money in less than a year and walk away, or try my new site but lose out on all these great offers.

Because I had so many eager buyers, it made me regret posting the site for sale, and I decided to keep it. I wanted to try launching my new site first, as I could always sell it later now that I knew there was a good market for it. I may even get higher offers in the future. I recently found an old email from September 2012 where a broker was offering the domain for sale for $150,000, and another email in May 2011 direct from the owner offering it to me for $200,000. In both these cases, it was just one domain on a big list of domains, so that is why I did not initially remember it. The point is that in 2011-2012, people seemed to think it was worth $100,000+ so there is no reason I could not try to get a high amount for it now. If anything, the video game industry has grown substantially since then, so the domain should be worth even more than it used to be.

Also, since 2008 when I sold Bored.com, I miss having a big popular site that generates a predictable cash flow, and I think GameReviews.com has the potential to be another site like that. I just need to figure out the best thing to do with it. You can see what I created so far by going to GameReviews.com. I collect video game reviews from over 100 other game sites and put them all on one constantly updated page. I also do the same with video game news, gaming videos, and gamer podcasts.

My Outsourcing Adventure

Everyone already knows about outsourcing, but I did something a little different than usual with it. Because I try to keep everything in my business as virtual as possible, having people do work remotely is a good fit. I have had very good experiences outsourcing work (programming, web design, accounting, etc.) through freelance sites.

I have never really done much with online outsourcing for my personal life though. There are sites that specialize in this, like TaskRabbit.com where local people do household errands and other items on your to-do list, and Fiverr.com where you can outsource small virtual tasks for as little as $5. It is just something I had never tried before. Then one day I happened to be reading an article about these sites, and it motivated me to try to solve a non-business problem I was having. In the past ten years, I have written over 100 songs as a hobby. The problem is that although I write good lyrics, I don't play any instruments and am a very bad singer, so it is frustrating not to be able to turn my lyrics into nice sounding songs. I recorded most of my songs by playing around with the instrumentals/beats that come built into my Casio keyboard and editing them into a backing track. This method of using pre-recorded music was limiting because it did not allow me to customize the songs at all.

Fiverr.com is filled with postings from musicians offering to create songs for you or to make your poems into songs. So I decided to have them turn some of my lyrics into songs (they created the melodies). The prices ranged from $5 to $55 per song. I liked most of the songs they made and thought I got great results for the small amount of money I spent, but I still wanted to hear what one of my songs would sound like if I could translate exactly what I hear in my head to actual music. On TV shows like *Nashville*, songwriters are always making demos of their songs, so I decided to take things to the next level and make a real demo. After doing a little Googling, I was able to find some recording studios that make demos remotely, so you don't have to physically be in their studio. You just email them your lyrics and a rough demo (I sang the melody into my iPhone), and they have their studio musicians record it.

I ended up going with HooHahSongDemos.com mainly because they offered a low price (around $365), and their songs sounded professional. The cost would actually have been $100 less if I had been able to give them a rough demo version of my song on keyboard or guitar, but since I could not do that, they told me I had to pay them extra for song writing assistance (co-writing). Ten days later they sent me the finished song. I was somewhat surprised because I was not aware they even had started working on it. The result was a mixture of good and bad. The good thing was that the song they created sounded like a real song on the radio. Very catchy, and not amateur like a homemade demo. The problem was that it did not sound much like the vocal demo I gave them. They changed the melody some and did the song at a much faster tempo, and by doing that they changed it from a sappy/emotional power ballad to a country rock song. I told them ahead of time what I was looking for, but I think because I was using their co-writing service (even though I didn't want to), they made it sound how they thought was best.

The problem was this was not really what I was looking for. The whole point was for me to showcase my songwriting, and translate what I heard in my head to a real song. When they changed it significantly, it really did not help me, even if their version was better. If I am not going to sing on it or play an instrument, I need it to sound at least how I envisioned it. Otherwise, it is not really my song anymore. All that being said, if I had just written the lyrics, but had no idea what music and melody to use for the song, I would have been extremely pleased with what they gave me. You can hear what they came up with on my site at MCEricB.com. The song is called *What If* (scroll down that song's page to the original version by Jonathan Wood).

Since that time, I have made much progress, but as with most things in life, it is a mixed bag. Instead of using a recording studio for my other songs, I started using musicians on Fiverr.com, but this time I created the melodies and gave them direction on how to make the music. On average it cost me $25 per song. I have had ten different Fiverr musicians record 50 songs for me so far, and I am very happy with the results. I just sing a demo into my iPhone and then email it to them along with the lyrics. Almost all the songs got just as good reviews as the one that had been professionally produced. You can hear them on my MCEricB.com site and see what you think. As an example, listen to my song *Father To A Son*.

Sometimes, little things make a big difference. I did not like around 20% of the songs that were created for me, so I was planning to have another performer redo them. Recently though, I realized that just changing the tempo of these songs totally fixes them. All I have to do is put the song into a free program I found named MP3 Speed), pick how much I want to slow down or speed up the song, and within seconds it gives me a revised MP3 file. The *Father To A Son* song above is an example of this (the original was too slow and sappy, so I sped it up).

Another example of how a small change can make a big difference is that I paid $5 to have a Fiverr producer do a dance remix of *What If* (the recording studio song), to make it more modern sounding, and it came out great (you can hear it on the top of the *What If* page).

So, all that is the good part. The bad part is that based on my experience, and other musicians I have talked to, it is very hard to make any money or even get people to hear your songs. I don't even try to sell my music, it is all free, and I still hardly have any listeners. I put all my songs on my own site, which has ads on it, but so far that has made no money. I also upload all my songs to SoundCloud.com, ReverbNation.com, and Soundclick.com, but most of the time they only get one or two listens a month. I tried using ReverbNation's Digital Distribution service for one of my songs, and that puts it on over 30 online music sites such as Spotify.com and Rdio.com, where I get a small fee every time it is played (no income yet). It also places it for sale for 99 cents on iTunes, Google Play, and Amazon.com, but it has not had any sales yet.

For each of my songs, I pay $9.95 to use ReverbNation's Crowd Review, where 20 random people listen to my song and write a short review of it. I love this service, and I also put these these reviews on my website. I thought adding that unique content (over 1,000 reviews so far) would help increase my site's search engine ranking to get more traffic (and ad income), but it has had zero effect.

I also have tried advertising my songs. Sites such as SoundClick.com have an automated system, where for $10-$30 for 24 hours, I can pay to be featured as the song of the day in certain categories, or I can have a banner ad for my song run throughout the site. This helps the song rank higher on their charts, which in turn can lead to even more listens. I tried it for several songs, and they did get to #1 on the charts, but there was not much extra action for the songs once the ads ran out, so it was not worth it.

Normally a songwriter like myself would start playing at clubs, bars, and coffee houses to build a following to promote CD sales and to help get a record deal. I am not a musician and can't do that, so I am stuck. The good thing though is that songwriting is just a hobby for me; I am not trying to make a living from it, so I don't need it to be a success. It just is frustrating that it is so hard to get my songs heard.

Illegal Sites

If you are a small company, it is important to do whatever you can not to get sued. A lawsuit will eat up all your time and money, even if you think you did nothing wrong. I am frequently presented with business opportunities that would probably make a good profit, but I avoid them because there is too big a risk of getting in trouble. Here are some examples and some things to watch out for:

1. **Media sites** - Sites that let you watch free TV shows, free movies, or listen to free songs online. Several major lawsuits by record companies, TV networks, and movie studios made it illegal to create a site that links to pirated/illegal content, even if you don't host any of the content on your server. There are some ways of doing it legally though, like by linking to content on sites such as Youtube.com or Hulu.com, which have systems for detecting copyrighted content.

2. **Celebrity-related sites** - Celeb gossip and fan sites usually get a lot of traffic, but most of them are using illegal content. For one thing, all the celebrity photos are copyrighted by the photographer or agency. Then on top of that, on a fan site, the website owner is making money from the celebrity's name and image without compensating the celebrity, which can be illegal.

3. **Pre-made sites and databases** - For $25-$100, it is easy to buy a pre-built site that offers free recipes, jokes, funny videos, etc. The webmaster creates these sites ahead of time and sells multiple copies of them, so that is why they are cheap. In

general this is a good deal if you are looking for a low-cost way to start a network of sites, but be aware that sometimes that content is copied illegally from other sites. For example, if you buy a recipe site with 40,000 recipes for $100, you can't expect that the webmaster thought of all those recipes him or herself. He obviously copied them from other sites, or all from one big site. There are a lot of legal and moral gray areas when it comes to this sort of thing, and most of the time it works out fine, but just be aware there could be potential problems. For example, I had to shut down my site that analyzed peoples' dreams, because the dream database I bought many years prior turned out to be copied from another site, and I could not find a different database to buy to replace it. The same thing happened with a smilies (little smiley face graphics) site I bought. I also once had to redo the graphics on a site I purchased because another webmaster told me the site design was copied from his site. It is very rare these small situations ever lead to lawsuits, but you need to realize that if another website (or their lawyer) contacts you about something like this, they are probably right about it.

4. **Celebrity domain names** - It is usually illegal for you to own a domain name that has a celebrity's name in it, like britney-spears.com. This is a violation of their trademark, and in some cases is even considered cybersquatting, which can in extreme cases be punishable by jail time. Usually, they just take the domain name away from you. Even bidding on trademarked search terms in a search engine to get traffic to your site can be illegal.

5. **Typo domain names** - If you own a domain name that is a typo of a famous brand or company (such as pepsy.com), and you don't have a legitimate reason for having it (like it is your last name, or you owned it before the big company or brand became famous), there is a good chance it will eventually get taken away from you, and you may even get sued.

6. **Sites with user uploaded content** - If you create a site that lets users upload videos, photos, or songs, you are opening yourself up to the risk of a big lawsuit. Many websites have been put out of business by lawsuits from giant companies with teams of lawyers that sue if your users post content that violates their copyrights. Youtube.com was sued for this, in a $1 billion lawsuit filed by Viacom (owner of MTV, Paramount Pictures, Comedy Central, etc.). And, years ago, a large website named Bolt.com was put out of business from their users posting copyrighted music videos. Don't think you are protected just because you are not posting the content to your site yourself.

7. **Email marketing** - You can get into major trouble for sending spam-type emails to promote your site, and you can even get into trouble by paying another company to do it for you. Aside from legal problems, there is a very good chance upset recipients will complain to your web host, and your web host will shut your site down. Even if the email list you used was opt-in, if it results in complaints, your site can get shut down. Your web host won't care if you did things correctly or not. Another problem is that many companies that say they use only opt-in email lists don't really use them or are not careful about

their opt-out methods, resulting in complaints from recipients.

8. **Brokerage Sites** - Certain types of sites require state licenses, like if you are selling or brokering concert tickets, boats, or real estate. Another example is that there are all sorts of federal and state laws when it comes to giving out loans or providing escrow services. The vast majority of websites don't need to worry about this issue, but it is something to keep in mind.

9. **Sales Tax** - If you are running an e-commerce site (online store), make sure you charge sales tax. You need to register as a business in your state and get set up with the state's sales tax department. Also, there are new laws that make it so that if you have sales in other states, you will need to pay sales tax to those states, so make sure to check on that.

10. **Unlicensed images** - Many people think it is OK to copy photos from Google image search or other sites, but it isn't. Almost all images you would want to use are copyrighted. Even if you remotely load the images (embed them) from the source site, and don't host them yourself, it is still illegal. For several blogs that I purchased, I received copyright infringement lawsuit threats from lawyers over photos the sites were using. I settled each of them for $200-$2,000 and then sold the sites.

Most of the time, the types of legal problems I have discussed here are easily resolved without the website owner getting into much trouble. In my 20 years in business, I have never been sued or had to use a lawyer. For the first 5-10 years, I did not worry too much as I did not have a lot to lose. It is only once I became a big company that I started to play it safe because I knew it would be more worthwhile for people to sue me.

Amazon Mechanical Turk

Back in 2005, Amazon.com launched a website called Mechanical Turk. It is a posting board for small tasks that people can do from home, such as writing reviews, transcribing podcasts, describing photographs, answering surveys, etc. These tasks have nothing to do with Amazon.com; Amazon just runs the site. Workers are usually paid $.01-$.20 for each task.

The name "Mechanical Turk" comes from "The Turk," a fake chess-playing machine from the 1700s. The owners presented it as being 100% automated, fooling celebrities such as Benjamin Franklin and Napoleon Bonaparte, but decades later it was exposed as a hoax. It was actually an illusion, with a human chess master hiding inside.

The Amazon service has attracted a good following, so I decided to give it a try (as an employer) for three jobs:

1. Give comments/feedback about my virtual pets website at Adoptme.com - 50 cents each.

2. Tell me a true story from your life, such as getting a job, buying a house, getting fired, going on a date, traveling, experiencing money problems or an embarrassing moment, going fishing, etc., to be posted on a new site I am creating - 10 cents each.

3. Give comments/feedback about my discount flower delivery website at CheapFlowers.com – 20 cents each.

After 5-10 minutes of setting up my account, depositing money, and configuring the postings, I was up and running. I made it so there was a limit of 50 responses for each job. I had no idea if what people wrote would be any good or if it would all be junk, but I was happy with the results. A lot of workers did submit fake content, it was either total gibberish or they copied the content from another site, so you need to carefully review all the submissions and reject the bad ones. What was left after that was good though.

My Adoptme.com and CheapFlowers.com sites were both created in the early 2000s and looked very outdated, so that is why I wanted user feedback on them. I emailed all the comments people made to my graphics designer, who used those comments to create new versions of these sites. Mechanical Turk can be used for more complicated projects than what I did, but I chose these three projects because I just wanted to get familiar with the system. I plan to post more projects to Mechanical Turk in the future.

Fake Passwords

I have a webmaster secret that I will reveal here. As far as I know, I was the first (and maybe only) webmaster to have ever done this. Here it is:

Almost everybody has used a site where you get a username and password, but you probably don't know what a pain it is to run a site like that. Aside from the programming involved in setting up the system that gives out usernames and passwords, the main problem is that users constantly forget their login info. And, if you set it up so they can email themselves the lost password, many times that email gets deleted as spam by their spam filter, or they have changed their email address. Another problem is hackers, who can easily get into the site, and then post in various forums how they got in or post a username and password for other people to use.

If you run a pay site, then all of these customer login problems become your problem. If a customer can't log in, they will want to cancel or even worse they will dispute the charge with their credit card company. No matter what, just dealing with the emails and phone calls for lost passwords is a lot of work.

So, after a few years of doing things the normal way, I decided to change all my membership sites to use a fake login system. I had my programmer make it so that no matter what username and password the customer entered, it would let them in. And, to keep things simple, when they signed up I gave all the customers the same username and password. That way if anybody ever emailed me saying they lost their login info, I would instantly know what it was without having to look it up.

For example, FindCash.com allowed people to check to see if they were owed unclaimed money by the government. If they were, I charged them $10 for a username and password to find out how much they were owed and how to collect it. When I switched from using real logins to fake ones, I was worried customers would catch on and that a lot of people would just get in for free instead of paying. Or, maybe somebody would post on a forum that everybody could get into my site for free, and it would get overloaded. But, none of that ever happened. After I made the change, I did not notice any decrease in sales, and the customer login problems stopped.

Another trick I used was that I told customers their membership was only good for 30 days, but that was not really true. Since all the logins were fake, I could not track their membership time, so they actually had unlimited access to the site. Although I only charged a one-time fee for the site, I did not want to advertise unlimited access because I was worried some customers would do a huge number of searches and crash my database. Luckily that never happened.

These solutions worked great, but mainly they are a good example of how thinking outside the box can sometimes lead to good solutions. The Internet is still young and there frequently is no "right way" to do things. Sometimes you have to improvise as you go along.

What Is The Next Big Thing?

The cryptocurrency business (Bitcoin and other electronic currencies) feels a lot like the Internet did back in 1995. Everybody was talking about it, but most people had no idea how to use it, or go about setting up a website. It was obvious it had big growth potential though. Also, the Internet back then had a hacker feel, just like cryptocurrency currently does.

One of the good things about Bitcoin is that you don't really need to know how it works to use it, just like when you visit a website you don't need to know about the server, database, programming, web host, and webmaster. Bitcoin is an electronic form of payment, similar in a way to how you can send and receive money using Paypal, Western Union, or a bank wire. It is just a much cheaper and more anonymous way of doing it, like in the late 1990s when Napster was a novel and free way to download music. Napster relied on the users' PCs to host the files (peer-to-peer file sharing); Bitcoin relies on a publicly distributed database of transactions (known as the "block chain") hosted on thousands of nodes (computers) throughout the world.

It took me many months to get around to setting up my CheapFlowers.com site to accept Bitcoin. I knew it would be a long, complicated process, and I was unsure if there was even much benefit in doing it (surprisingly, I ended up getting extra sales). The early days of the Internet were also not very user-friendly, but that soon changed. I expect the same thing to happen with cryptocurrencies.

After 20 years in the website/domain business, I am eager to try something new. I would never go back to trying to make money offline, but there is much more to the Internet than just building websites. Cryptocurrency is one of the few opportunities I have been excited about, in terms of the money-making potential. Other big technologies have emerged over the years, but they just weren't right for me:

- **Web Phone Calls and Video Calls** - I tried making phone/video calls back in 1999, but the whole thing was just awful, especially on dial-up Internet. And, most recipients did not have the ability or know-how to take the calls. Skype eventually became popular as the technology improved, but the company was losing lots of money until Microsoft bought them.

- **Online Videos** - Back in the late 90s, I watched some music videos by downloading the files from a website, and it was absolutely amazing. But, it was torture downloading the huge files on dial-up, and streaming them was too slow. I knew online videos were the future, but there was not much to do about it. In 2006, Youtube became a hit, but they had huge losses due to server/bandwidth costs, and might have gone out of business had they not been bought out by Google.

- **Mobile Apps** - Mobile was an obvious growth area when smartphones started getting popular. Even before the iPhone, the industry was taking off, but there was no easy way to capitalize on that. I could have made a ton of apps like I churned out websites, but I am not sure those apps would have done any better than my websites. Also, I used a Blackberry for many years, which was limiting. I was not an expert on apps and what mobile phone users needed, because all I did was use it to check my email.

- **Social Networks** - I could tell this would be a big business, but it was not something I was personally into at the time. Sites like Friendster and Myspace eventually failed, so it turned out not to be a great business for anyone other than Facebook.

- **The Cloud** - It is basically just Web Hosting 2.0. The differences between cloud hosting and old-fashioned web hosting are way more technical than what the vast majority of customers want to know. It basically boils down to that cloud hosting is a better way to host your website or data. Everything is moving to the cloud not because it is something new, but due to it being much cheaper and easier than the alternatives (like having your own data center). That is all great for the customer, but the problem is that running a cloud hosting company is still just as much hassle as running a regular hosting company. There are non-stop technical problems and complaints from customers. Plus, the technology is constantly changing, so you need to always be investing time and money in new equipment and software while the prices for your service go lower and lower. Of course, there are other ways to be in the cloud business without being a web host, but those opportunities are not that different from what was out there when just regular hosting was available.

- **3D Printers** - Many people think printing items/products in your home will disrupt the entire manufacturing industry. That may be, but it involves complex things like blueprints, CAD/CAM, engineering, product design, and manufacturing, all of which are areas I am not that knowledgeable about or interested in.

- **Virtual Reality** - Oculus Rift (VR headsets) was recently bought by Facebook for $2 billion, and Google Glass (augmented reality glasses) type products will soon be available to everyone, so this business is set to explode. I look forward to trying these devices myself, but it all based on complex programming and expensive hardware, so it is not an easy market to enter. I did test the waters back in 2009 by creating an augmented reality area (at a cost of around $1,000) on my Adoptme.com website. Users could print out the page and then, using their webcam, watch an Adoptme pet come to life on their desk. Hardly anybody used it though.

Online payment systems and currencies, on the other hand, are something much more up my alley. I dabbled in that business when I started Digicredit.com 15 years ago and have an extensive background in finance (stock market, bonds, options, etc.). I am not sure Bitcoin is the future, but there seems to be a lot of opportunity there.

Bitcoin 2.0

While Bitcoin adoption spreads around the Internet, some forward thinkers have already left Bitcoin in the dust and are building "Bitcoin 2.0." Here are some of the more interesting new cryptocurrency-related technologies:

- **Ripple** - A peer-to-peer payment network that is a cross between Facebook, Paypal, and Western Union. It supports almost any currency or commodity and has almost no fees.

- **Colored Coins** - Uses "sidechain" technology, allowing you to mark Bitcoins with additional information so they can be used to trade more than just currency. You "color" each coin to represent one of your assets such as a car, house, gold, stock, bond, etc. Anyone can then trade these colored coins anywhere, just like how Bitcoin works. It also has the security of piggybacking on the existing Bitcoin network and protocol.

- **Ethereum** - Allows financial contracts on top of its cryptocurrency, kind of like an automated escrow service. Each Ethereum transaction is recorded in the Ethereum cryptoledger and can have its own scripting code (providing the automation part).

- **Omni Layer (and also Counterparty)** - Uses the Bitcoin block chain to store data, so it has the security of Bitcoin, but creates a different currency than Bitcoin. The extra data can be used to create smart contracts to enable the electronic exchange of assets such as stocks, bonds, real estate, and intellectual property. In addition, you can create your own currency with it.

- **Open Transactions** - An open-source financial cryptography software that can be used to create an online financial market and banking system. You can also use it to create your own cryptocurrency backed by hard assets such as gold, silver, dollars, euros, stocks, oil futures, and more. In addition, it can be used for purposes such as issuing stock, virtual currencies for online games, paying dividends, sending and receiving digital cash, and escrow using scripted custom agreements.

- **Coinffeine** - A game-theory-based Bitcoin exchange (a place where people buy and sell their Bitcoin, kind of like a stock exchange). There are no fees because it is peer-to-peer (from one person to another person, with no central intermediary). The "game theory" part involves a zero-trust exchange algorithm that forces users to cooperate in several micro-transactions until the entire transaction is complete. If users pull out of the transaction early, they lose money.

- **HolyTransaction** - A universal cryptocurrency wallet. Typically if you want to buy ten different cryptocurrencies (Bitcoin, LiteCoin, Dogecoin, NameCoin, etc.) you need to have ten different wallets, which makes it hard to manage. HolyTransaction solves this problem, plus it comes with currency exchange features so you can easily convert one cryptocurrency to another.

- **Crypto::Stocks** - A crowdfunding site that operates like a stock exchange for cryptocurrency companies. Unlike traditional crowdfunding sites where consumers pre-order a product or provide loans or venture capital to a business, at

CryptoStocks.com people invest Bitcoin in companies to make money via dividends that are paid out in Bitcoin. You can also speculate by buying and selling shares, as each stock is traded like a "real" public company. There are possible legal problems with all of this though. A lot of it depends on the laws in your particular country (For example, in the USA, much of this probably violates SEC rules).

- **NXT** - An improved version of Bitcoin, written entirely from scratch in Java. It has all the abilities of Bitcoin, but also can handle colored coins, includes a decentralized asset exchange (i.e., you can buy and sell things with no 3rd party needed), includes a built-in encrypted messaging system, and has the ability for anonymous payments. It also uses much less electricity for mining than Bitcoin does (it can be mined using a mobile phone, Raspberry Pi, or any PC), due to the use of "proof-of-stake" instead of "proof-of-work" protocol.

Keep in mind the industry is in its infancy. Unlike the Internet back when it first started to take off, the currency market is not something totally new. It took many years for the Internet to really catch on, due to slow dial-up access, ineffective search engines, complex web hosting, expensive programming costs, and lack of great content. Cryptocurrency, on the other hand, is disrupting the already existing financial markets. The foreign exchange market (people converting money from one currency to another to make payments) alone has over $5 trillion a day in volume, and that does not include the millions of dollars a day that is transferred within each country via wire transfers, ACH, and services such as Western Union and Paypal. Add to that the $500 billion a day traded on the global stock and commodity markets, and this total dwarfs the amount of business that is done on the Internet. This means there are fortunes to be made in cryptocurrency just by grabbing even a very small slice of the financial market economy.

Flipping Websites

If you want to buy and sell websites, there is only one main place to do it: Flippa.com. They are like the eBay of website sales. Over the years, I have bought and sold around 100 websites on Flippa, starting back when it was just a section on the SitePoint.com forum named SitePoint Marketplace. In 2009, it spun-off into a separate website, and they added a lot more features. What is amazing is that they never have had any real competition.

Personally, I have not found buying or selling websites on Flippa to be very profitable, but at least it is easy to do. Many of the sites being sold are good deals, because the owners are selling for a legitimate reason, like they need cash for an emergency, they got a full-time job and no longer have time to run the site, they are having health problems and can't run the site any longer, or they can't handle the web hosting. I did not have any sites I bought where the seller was trying to scam me, although I know that does happen. On average, I would say the sites I bought made less income than the sellers claimed they were making (none ever made more), and traffic generally went down in the year after I bought them. Almost every site was a big project to move to my server, so I highly recommend trying to take over the seller's web hosting account if possible. That way you don't have to deal with moving the site, or at least not right away. Also, I would often ask the seller to change the ads on the site to use my ad code instead of theirs. Otherwise, by the time I moved the site to my server and figured out the programming enough to know how to change the ads, many weeks would pass (with the income going to the seller). If you have a talent fixing up sites and getting traffic to them, then you could make a lot of money flipping sites on Flippa. It is just not something that I was good at. I was an expert at the technical and business parts of taking over the sites, but not at adding value to them.

Here's an example of a Flippa.com deal. In 2012, I paid $120,000 for 14 article-type Wordpress sites from various different sellers. These sites had thousands of custom written articles, and I added several thousand more over the next two years. The largest of the sites was TipTopTens.com, which was making a profit of around $3,000/month at the time I bought it. I ended up auctioning off all these sites as one big package on Flippa in 2014 for $11,600.

To sell a site, Flippa charges a $19 listing fee (only $9 for domains) plus a 10% commission if it sells. Flippa uses an auction format, although you can also have a fixed "Buy It Now" price. The sites I have tried to sell received bids much lower than I hoped for, but if I were desperate for cash, at least I would be able to sell the sites to somebody. I have never had much luck trying to sell sites on my own, and there are very few brokers who sell sites, so using Flippa is the best option.

More recently, Flippa has started to handle a large number of domain name sales. Because Flippa uses auctions (which have a limited duration), the sales prices of their domains are usually lower than those sold by domain brokers, so there are some good deals to be found for buyers. Also, I am not sure of the stats for website sales, but many Flippa domain sales are negotiated after the auction ends unsold, when the seller is more desperate and willing to accept a lower price. So, just because a domain does not get sold, don't give up, and make the seller an offer instead. As a domain seller, Flippa is not usually the first place I try to sell my domains, but it certainly is an option worth trying. Because you can set a hidden reserve price (the minimum you would sell it for), you have nothing to lose other than the $9 listing fee per domain.

Viral Videos (The Story of "Pimp My Sleigh")

In 2006, I decided to take a shot at creating a viral video, to get extra traffic to Bored.com (and maybe get mentioned on TV, put in a movie, given a record deal, or any of the other fun things that viral videos tend to lead to). I had written songs before, but hadn't tried to do anything commercial with them, and had never made any videos.

As I am a bad singer and don't have a lot of musical talent, I figured writing a funny Christmas song would be the way for me to go, as people tend to pass that kind of thing around during the holidays. And, unlike normal songs that usually die a quick death, holiday songs are played over and over again, year after year. *Pimp My Ride* (the MTV show where they made boring cars look spectacular) was popular and all sorts of other things were suddenly getting "pimped," so I decide to write a song about Santa Claus called *Pimp My Sleigh*. After several days of writing (whenever I was not working - in the car, waiting in line, eating, etc.), I completed my masterpiece and was eager for people to hear it.

For most of my hip-hop songs, I create the music myself, but for this one I needed it to sound more professional, and also "Christmasy," and I had no idea how to make a Christmas sounding beat. So, I searched in Google and found a bunch of musicians who advertised that they created custom beats, and I emailed them about my project. I ended up paying $100 for one of them to do it for me. I made a vocals-only recording of the song, and they used that to make the music for it. I then re-recorded the vocals over their music.

My next step was to search the Web for animators who had experience creating musical animations. I emailed the song to a few of them and ended up giving the project to an animator who was just launching his business. He created the Flash video for me for only $250 because it was good exposure for his company and he knew the video would get a lot of views. You can watch *Pimp My Sleigh* on my site at MCEricB.com or on YouTube.com.

By the time everything was done, it was already the beginning of December, so after showing the video to my friends and family, I immediately added it to the top of Bored.com. I also uploaded it to YouTube and a few other video sites. The response was great, and YouTube viewers gave it high ratings. I was ready to hire an agent and prepare for my world tour, but nothing ever happened. Sadly, my video did not go viral. Yes, over 500,000 people saw the video on Bored.com, another few hundred thousand watched it on YouTube, and a few sites and blogs linked to it, but it never really caught on. It did not take the leap from being popular to something viral.

Now, every year as Christmas time comes around, a little bit of hope awakens in me, knowing that my video has yet another chance at success. This at least gives me some solace. My story does not end there though. I figured the more holiday videos I made, the more entries I would get into the viral video lottery, so I wrote some additional holiday-type songs, all with music videos:

Hip Hop Hanukkah - Not everybody celebrates Christmas, so I wanted to try to reach as large an audience as possible by covering both holidays.

Party On Your Birthday - Birthdays are such a big market, so I figured there must be room for more than just the traditional *Happy Birthday To You* song, especially a more modern version. Also, many people do not know this, but the *Happy Birthday* song is actually covered by copyright so many public performances of it are actually illegal (singing it in your home to friends and family is legal, using it in a TV show or movie without permission is not).

The TurboTax Rap - TurboTax software held a contest for people to make a music video about using TurboTax to do your income taxes (I have been a TurboTax user for many years), and this was my entry. I didn't win, but a lot of people saw the video on the TurboTax website and Youtube.

These videos got some good reviews, but none of them reached the tipping point and went viral. Based on those results, I have pretty much given up on the viral video dream. I did try one new tactic, though, where instead of making videos for the masses, I made some specifically for a few of my websites, in the hopes the videos would bring in some extra traffic:

CheapFlowers.com Rap - I did this song as a demo, hoping I would have somebody else record a real version, but I never got around to getting that done, so eventually I just added it to my CheapFlowers.com website.

The Water Tower Rap - I think I created the first song ever written about water towers (for my WaterTowers.com site), and certainly the first rap about them.

I'm A Pig - A kids song I created for my iAnimals.com website (I no longer own the site).

I'm A Horse - Another kids song I created for iAnimals.com.

Over the years, I have also added animated songs written and sung by another musician (I paid him for it) to my sites:

AdoptMe Music Videos - Songs performed by the virtual pets that you can adopt at AdoptMe.com.

Rapping Babies - Songs performed by the virtual babies that you can adopt at CyberInfants.com.

So far neither the songs I created myself, nor the ones I paid someone else to perform, have brought any extra visitors to the sites. They were fun projects to work on, but from a business standpoint they have been a complete waste of time and money.

Partnerships

I have been involved in several partnerships, and none of them have ever worked out very well. I previously wrote about how I got my AdoptMe plush toy sold at Toys"R"Us. As I mentioned in that chapter, this was a partnership. For many years I had run the Adoptme.com website and made no money from it, so one of my business associates suggested we do a partnership where he would sell AdoptMe merchandise. I agreed, as I had no interest in doing anything that was not 100% virtual. The only condition I imposed was that no matter what happened with the toy company, I would still end up with the Adoptme.com website. That way I had nothing to lose.

Our main product was the Adoptme Plush Toy, which allowed kids to play with the pets they adopted both online and offline. Inside each box was a personalized code the buyer could redeem on the Adoptme.com website to adopt a virtual version of their plush toy. The product was great, and users loved it, but the main problem was it took us three years to get to the point where we were actually selling it. Over that three year period we spent a lot of money and effort getting the product to market, so by the time it was sold in stores, we were out of funds and needed to move on. Our only hope was for it to be a smash hit, but it wasn't. We sold a few a day from the Adoptme.com website, and it sold well in some stores, but it cost us $700/month for product liability insurance, plus the cost of a small office and the salary for a part-time employee, so it was not worth keeping the company going unless we could get an investor. We tried that but were unsuccessful, so we shut the company down.

An interesting issue that came up when dealing with Toys"R"Us, was that if the toy became popular, we did not have the money to fund the manufacturing costs for big orders that Toys"R"Us would give us. With the two month overseas shipping time and then another 1-2 months to get paid from Toys"R"Us, we would have had to put up a lot of cash in advance for each order. Yes, we could have used a factoring company (they buy your invoices at a discount giving you instant cash), but that would have taken away much of our profit.

Back to the issue of partnerships though. The problem I have had with all my partnerships is that they end up taking much longer than expected to get going, and this creates the need for extra money to keep things running. Our biggest expense and delay with Adoptme Toys was that we paid $7,000 to a manufacturing broker to help us get the product manufactured cheaply overseas, and that was a total disaster. We did this because we had heard horror stories about dealing with overseas factories, so we thought using an expert would be a good idea. The broker hooked us up with a factory that ended up screwing us, so we wasted $7,000 and one and a half years.

We then had to get started with a totally new factory in China, and it took two months for them to ship us each order (by boat). We started with a very small order to make sure the toys came out okay, so by the time we made some changes and placed a larger order and received it, almost a year had passed. All this extra time was eating up money, so my partner and I both had to put up more money or else the company would have gone out of business. I put around $37,000 total into this toy business, plus the $75,000 or so it cost me to originally develop the Adoptme.com website. For two years, I also had one of my employees work almost full-time on the Adoptme Toys project, which hurt my company. When my partner eventually kicked in some extra money, we had this employee leave my company and work for Adoptme Toys.

Back when I started the partnership, I had considered things like this might happen, but I figured no matter what I would get the Adoptme.com website back, so it would not be a big problem. Things never work out that simple though. It was now three years later, and my partner had invested a lot of money in the business. His goal was to try to sell the Adoptme Toys company, which included the Adoptme.com website, to try to recover some of the money we each invested. The problem was that while we might have sold it for enough to pay us both back, I would then lose the website that I had spent $75,000 to develop, so I would not get any of that investment returned to me.

Luckily, my partner could not find a buyer easily, so I stepped in and offered $25,000 to buy the Adoptme.com website back. Because he had no other options, he accepted. So, in addition to spending $37,000 in unplanned cash towards the partnership, I now had to spend another $25,000 just to get back the website that was originally mine and that I never was supposed to have lost.

In the end I did get a toy produced and sold in stores, and there was always a chance it could have been a big hit (like Webkinz soon became), so I don't regret giving it a try. That is the nature of being an entrepreneur. Sometimes you win, sometimes you lose.

But, the Adoptme story does not end there. There was a surprising twist that I will write about in the next chapter.

Partnerships – Part II

In the previous chapter, I talked about the partnership I was involved in to sell Adoptme plush toys. The toy company went out of business, and I ended up losing the $37,000 I had invested plus I paid another $25,000 to buy the Adoptme.com website back. Nine months after we shut down the toy company, my ex-employee who had been spending almost all his time on Adoptme Toys, emailed me to ask about buying Adoptme.com. He had moved to China and was interested in resurrecting AdoptMe Toys to sell them in Asia. As he now lived where they would be manufactured, it would make things much easier for him. He also had investors. Because virtual pets are huge in Asia, it was not as difficult for him to raise money there.

He offered me $85,000, but I had already spent $75,000 to develop Adoptme.com, $37,000 on the partnership, and $25,000 on buying back the Adoptme.com website, so I told him the lowest I would sell it for was $125,000. He agreed, but then said he needed up to three months to raise the money. I did not have any other potential buyers, so I accepted those terms. The day after I signed this agreement with him, he asked me to write up some financial projections for his investors. I said how I made nothing from the site (after I bought the site back, I added pop-unders that made $300/month which exactly covered the hosting costs of the two dedicated servers). I also told him that if he sold child-related ads on the site he could probably make thousands a month. The Adoptme site was programmed in Flash and very complicated, so I never wanted to deal with adding advertisements to the site myself. Because he was asking me all these questions, I took a closer look and in 10 minutes was able to stick a banner ad on all the pages. Within hours I realized it was making revenue at a rate of $3,000/month. I had valued the site at $125,000 when it was making nothing, so now that it was making $36,000/year it was worth much more, but unfortunately I was under contract to sell it. A few people I talked to told me to back out of the contract, but I always stick to my word, so that was not an option for me.

Luckily, three months passed and the buyer was not able to come up with the money. I even gave him an extra month as he said he was close to getting it. After that, I never heard from him again. In the end, everything worked out well for me, but it was a crazy ride.

Partnerships – Part III

I know many big companies (Apple, Google, etc.) have been built through partnerships, but that is not something I will ever do again. Many people dislike partnerships because of potential personality or decision-making conflicts that can eventually ruin things. Or, they don't want to give up control to their partner. Those were not the problems I had. Almost every time, the problems were due to money issues.

Not all partnerships are the same of course, and what I have done may not represent typical partnerships, but for what it is worth, here is a summary of the partnerships I have been involved in over the past 15 years:

Adoptme Toys - As I described in the previous chapters, I lost around $62,000, plus three years' worth of time and effort working on it.

FindRentals.com - In 2001, I was approached by a business associate who wanted to start a vacation rentals website using my FindRentals.com domain name, which I was not using at the time. I made a deal with him where I contributed the domain and handled setting up the website and the hosting, and he handled all the sales and the business end of it. Everything went pretty well, where I got the site set up and he sold a bunch of listings, and it has grown year after year, at one point with a staff of around 25 people (many of them salespeople paid on commission). The site is a success, but I have not made any profit from it so far. In the nine years since we started FindRentals.com, I paid over $100,000 to my programmer to do work on it, plus monthly fees to the web host. And, I spent a huge amount of time working on the site, even more than on my own sites. The problem is that there is never any "extra" money for me to get paid. A few years ago my partner tried to buy me out (for the amount of money I put into the site), and made $28,000 in payments, but then stopped because he was low on cash. Even if he eventually goes through with it, I will have no profit and nothing to compensate me for all the time I put into it. And, I will have lost the FindRentals.com domain name. I would have been much better off just holding the domain, doing nothing with it for the past 14 years, and then selling it for a big profit.

Cyberworx - I started this company in 1999 with a friend of the family, who was entrepreneurial and tech-savvy, but did not know much about the Internet. The goal was to create the types of online businesses I would never start myself, like ones that needed an office and had a lot of customer service and all the unautomated things that I hate doing. Initially we created some sites, such as a college textbook price comparison search engine and a site that showed what items local stores had on sale. The problem was these sites were not making enough profit for my partner to live on. (I already had my own business so I did not need to make anything from Cyberworx in order to survive.) To keep things going, my partner requested that I loan money to the company to pay him a $3,000/month salary, so he did not have to shut things down and take another job. I agreed to do that under the condition that I get paid back out of future income. Eventually more revenue did start coming in (from BargainPrinting.com, an online printing service), and he opened an office and more websites were built, but the company still needed my $3,000/month to cover expenses. I also co-signed the lease for their New York City office space. Things grew even more, and it got to the point where I was loaning the company $10,000/month so it would not go out of business.

The main problem with this was that I was not looking to invest any money in anything. When I started the company with my partner, the whole point was that we would be 50/50 partners, and I would contribute the technical/web part but it would not involve cash. Over time I loaned $185,000 to the company to keep it from going under, and almost all of this was money I borrowed from credit lines and credit cards, some with interest rates as high as 24%. That means in addition to that $185,000, I also paid another $50,000-$75,000 in interest. To make things even worse, soon after, my own company had negative cash flow of around $20,000/month. I had no credit lines left to use to cover my losses because they were all used for my Cyberworx loans, so I came dangerously close to going out of business myself. To make up for the cash shortage, I had to liquidate a bunch of high-quality domain names that I did not want to sell. One of these domains was InsuranceQuotes.com, which in 2010 sold for $5.9 million (as part of a website).

None of the money I lent to Cyberworx led to me owning more of the company. I already owned 50% as a partner; the money was just a loan. The problem is that after 16 years, I have never received any profits as a partner, and I received only around $6,000 towards paying back the loan (with no payments in the past 10 years). Even though the company has had enough money to pay salaries to anywhere from 7-15 employees over the years and spend money on things like trade shows, health insurance for employees, office space, salaries for the other partners, and even summer interns, there is never any money "left over" to pay me. Something always comes up that is more important. I understand not getting a profit as a partner, since that is the risk I took getting involved, but I feel ripped off that no payments are being made to me on the $185,000 I lent the company. I did not lend this money as an investor or venture capitalist; I did it to keep the company from going under. Because they are still in business all these years later, I would think they would find some way to make payments to me.

Also, I spent a huge amount of time over the first few years helping my partner set up the Cyberworx websites and business. I spent just as much time on those projects as on my own sites. Imagine how much more money I would have made, had I spent that time buying more domains or setting up sites for myself. Even more importantly, if I had that $185,000 back and had not been forced to liquidate those domains, I am pretty sure I would not have sold Bored.com a few years later. I did not sell Bored.com because I got some wildly high price for it, or because I thought its profits would decline. I sold it only to have money in the bank. If I were getting monthly profits from being a partner in Cyberworx, plus payback of the loan, I would have had a lot more money in the bank and not felt the need to sell anything. Because of all of this, my dealings with Cyberworx have had a big impact on the path that my life has taken.

FindCash.com - In 1997, I had the idea to create a website for people to search and see if they were owed unclaimed money by the government. In the 1980s, I had some success earning finders' fees by locating people owed unclaimed money, so I had some experience in the business. Back in 1997, it was much harder and more expensive than it is now to put a big database online, but I decided to give it a try. The problem was that the government mostly did not offer the data in electronic format to the public, so I partnered with a guy who was selling CDROMs of this data. He knew nothing about websites; therefore, I made a 50/50 deal with him where he provided me with the data, and I handled the website and all the marketing and customer service.

I programmed the site in Cold Fusion, and it cost around $1,000/month for the hosting because the size of the database (now this can be handled for $25/month). FindCash.com allowed people to search for free to see if their name was on the unclaimed money list, but if they were, they would need to pay $10 to find out how much they were owed and how to collect it. Over the years, my partner and I averaged a profit of around $1,000/month each. He lucked out because he only had to collect new data once a year, and after a few years I was able to get much of the data myself once the sources converted to electronic format. He just sat back and collected the $1,000 monthly checks I sent him.

It was not his fault that I did all the work, but it was a lot of effort for the $1,000/month that I made from it. Like with any e-commerce site, there was customer service, fraud issues, server problems, database updates, search engine marketing, etc. Income had been steadily declining due to the government making unclaimed money data more readily available to the public for free online, so after 12 years I bought him out. I then changed the site so that after people did a free search, it showed them Google ads for other unclaimed money sites, instead of having them to pay $10 to sign up for mine. Amazingly, this earned just as much profit and made it so I had to do no work. Overall I am glad I did this partnership, but if I had enough money back in 1997, I would have been much better off paying my ex-partner a one-time licensing fee instead of partnering with him and paying him over $100,000 in profits.

SantaBot is Coming To Town

In a previous chapter, I wrote about my attempts to create viral videos (such as *Pimp My Sleigh*). Although they were popular, I never made any money from them. So, unlike with holiday videos, it is interesting that one of my holiday websites took off. I created SantaBot.com in December of 2005 to have a site where kids could chat live with Santa Claus (it was actually a 100% automated chat bot program). The first year was an experiment because I had no idea how kids would react to it or what kind of questions they would ask. Each day, I would review the log files of the conversations, and see what answers "Santa" gave that needed to be changed or improved. By the time Christmas was over, I had edited SantaBot enough so many of the kids thought they really were talking with Santa, and not just a computer.

By New Year's Day, traffic to the site had died down, and so I left the site alone and in 2006 it did fine with no adjustments needed. Then in December 2007, Microsoft came out with its own Santa Bot but had to shut it down because parents complained it talked dirty to kids. At first this was a problem for me also because it made parents take a closer look at my Santa Bot, and they then complained about some of the things it said. At least my version only said bad things if the user first said something bad (it basically would just repeat the bad thing back to the user). This did not worry me too much, but I did change a few responses to try to make it more child-friendly. So, disaster was avoided, and I moved on.

Then, in 2008, a funny thing happened. It seems that after the whole Microsoft debacle, the general public realized they could get G-rated chat bots to talk dirty, so people made a game out of it. They would post their illicit SantaBot.com chat logs to various forums for others to see and to try to top. Most people still use my site the intended way, but all the links to it caused my "Christmas" site to become a site people now use all year round. Another good thing about Santa Bot is that ad rates are much higher in December, which is when it gets the most traffic. I make 2-3 times as much per visitor during the holiday season because advertisers are much more eager to advertise.

After the success of Santa Bot, a few years ago I created God Chat (talk to God) and added it to my site at Dumb.com, and that has also been a big success. In the future, I may create some other chat bots, such as a TurkeyBot for Thanksgiving and a BunnyBot for Easter. I doubt those will be big hits, but it is not very hard for me create them now that I have the basic bot programming done.

I also created chatterbots at adoptme.com/chats.php for my AdoptMe.com site, where users can chat live with the virtual pets they adopt. They don't just chat with some random pet, they chat with their own pet, which knows the owner's name, its own name, the last time it was fed, the last time it was walked, how old it is, and other personalized info. Many of the kids think they are talking to real pets, or a real person pretending to be their pet.

The lesson to be learned from all of this, if there is any, is that as a webmaster you never know which sites will do well and which won't. I have created many great and innovative sites that never get any traffic, even though I was sure they would be a hit. Many Internet entrepreneurs spend years focusing on one big site (like Mark Zuckerberg with Facebook), but I have taken a different approach in creating hundreds of smaller sites, and hoping a few will do well. To me, each new site I create is like a lottery ticket, so the more tickets I have, the more likely I will hit it big.

How A Domain Name Sale Works

You might be wondering how I sell a domain name. Most of the time, the buyer looks me up as the owner (using the WHOIS system) and then emails me an offer. Many times they ask me to call them or they ask for my phone number, and I always respond by saying to just email me an offer instead. I hate negotiating by phone, plus I like having a record of the emails for future use. That way if the deal does not happen, and the same buyer contacts me again months or years later, I can then see what previous offers they made. Also, many times I have to do some research to figure out what price to charge for the domain, and I can't do that very well while talking on the phone to the buyer.

Deciding what price to sell the domain for is never easy. First, I usually get a free automated appraisal of the domain at Estibot.com. This is just a rough guide to the value though. I also look at comparable domain sales published on sites such as DNJournal.com, and look to see what type of offers I have had on the domain in the past. Sometimes a major factor is also how eager I am to get the cash. I have sold great domains for low prices because I was desperate for money, or to pay off high-interest credit card loans, or to fund some new business venture. Alternatively, if I am just going to stick the cash in the bank at today's low interest rates (less than 1%), then I have less motivation to sell.

Most of the time I will tell the buyer I don't have an official asking price for the domain and ask them to make me an offer. I do this because sometimes their initial offer may be higher than the price I was hoping to get. Even then, I usually ask for double what they offered, as a negotiating tactic. Once we agree on a price, the buyer has two options.

They can either Paypal or wire me the money and I will then transfer ownership of the domain to them, or they can use an escrow service like Escrow.com or eCOP.com. Using an escrow service takes almost all the risk out of the transaction. If the buyer does not use escrow and instead pays me up front, they take the risk that I won't give them the domain as promised and then they will lose their money. Much like how a lawyer handles a real estate deal, domain escrow eliminates this risk by holding the buyer's money in a special account and not paying it to the seller until the buyer verifies they have ownership of the domain. The fee for domain escrow depends on the purchase price but is usually around $50-$100.

Another way to sell a domain is using a lease with an option to buy. I keep ownership of the domain, and the buyer pays me monthly payments, but I give them control of the domain so they can use it. I also give them an option to buy at a specific price so that way they don't have to worry about wasting time and money setting up their website and then having me not renew their lease.

Sometimes instead of a lease, I use an installment sale. This works pretty much the same way as a lease (monthly payments), but the contract is to buy the domain not just lease it. I don't charge any interest, and I don't charge a penalty if the buyer backs out. If they stop making payments, the contract is canceled, and the domain reverts back to me (it is already in my account so I have no risk). It is really no different than a lease, but most people like the idea better that they are "buying" it.

A lease or installment sale allows the buyer to start their website with much less risk. They get to use a great domain for their business, but if after a year or two they are not making money, they can decide to stop the payments. All they will have lost is the small amount they paid so far.

An example of this is the sale of my Heels.net domain. The buyer has a business named Heels Coaching that offers life coaching services to women. We settled on a price of $10,000 with $1,000 down and the rest due in 2 years, with the domain held in escrow at eCOP.com. The $10,000 price was higher than I would have expected to get from a cash sale, so even if there was only a 50/50 chance of her paying the balance at the end of two years, it was worth it for me. Also, worst case scenario, I would make $1,000 over the next two years, which was much better than the zero dollars in parking income I was currently getting from it. After two years, it turns out she decided to use the domain HeelsCoaching.com for her site instead, but I was fine with that. In fact, I think it was a good decision. She got to test out my domain and saved $9,000 once she realized it was not a good fit for her.

Here are some other examples of domains that I financed and then took back:

VisitRome.com - $37,000 price, payments of $750-$2,000 month over several years. The buyer paid for the first three years, then stopped.

GetVisibility.com - $3,000 price, $300 down, balance due in one year. The buyer only paid the down payment.

BuyLingerie.com - $20,000 price, $1,000 down, $100/month for two years with the balance due at the end of two years. The buyer paid for about a year but then stopped.

One thing to consider when leasing/financing a domain, is that because the domain is still listed with you as the owner, you are legally responsible for anything that happens, so you need to make sure the buyer is not using the domain for anything illegal. I have a clause in the domain leasing/financing contract I use that addresses this.

Some Bitcoin 2.0 Business Ideas

You still may be having a hard time wrapping your head around Bitcoin, and may be even more confused by Bitcoin 2.0. Over the last few years, cryptocurrency programmers have perfected and tested the Bitcoin model, but it leaves some people wanting more. Other cryptocurrencies have been able to piggyback on the Bitcoin architecture, or create a new but similar architecture of their own and offer all sorts of additional features. These features are like an extra dimension for the coin, giving it the power of a regular Bitcoin-type currency but also allowing extra information to be attached to it.

To help you better understand the possibilities, I will give you some real-life examples of what can be done:

- I could create my own currency called ImpulseCoin (my company is named Impulse Communications, Inc.). I could try to get people to use it, and if it were listed on some of the cryptocurrency exchanges, a market would develop for it. I could also make it a virtual currency on some of my sites. Like on my virtual pet site at Adoptme.com, I could give it out as rewards for special achievements and allow people to buy it to get a premium level Adoptme.com account that would unlock certain features on the site (or maybe people could use it to buy food or clothes for their virtual pets). Much like when a company goes public on the stock market, I would keep a certain amount of ImpulseCoins for myself, and then I could sell them later for a profit once there is a stable market for the coin.

- A site like Domaining.com (a source for domain industry news) could create a DomainingCoin and give it out to bloggers for each blog posting that gets published on Domaining.com. Domaining.com would then accept DomainingCoins as one of the payment options for Domaining.com ads, Domaining.com memberships, eCop.com escrow fees, and Lend.me domain loan listing fees. Because this would instantly give DomainingCoins some real value, a market might develop for them, and other domain-related sites also might start accepting them. For example, maybe I would sell one of my domains for DomainingCoins (instead of US Dollars), knowing I could use them to advertise on Domaining.com or sell them on a cryptocurrency exchange.

- Some small companies are crowdfunding by selling "shares" using these advanced cryptocurrencies. You are not usually selling ownership like with a stock; instead you are selling a percentage of the profits from your business. I could, for example, create a domain name cryptocoin, where I sell a profit share in one of my domains. Since I am trying to sell the domain Telemarketers.com right now, I could create TelemarkersCoin and offer a profit share of all proceeds over $25,000 (my goal would be $50,000) that I receive for it when I sell it. If I don't sell it by X date or sell it for higher than $25,000, I would need to pay some sort of penalty that would be distributed to coin holders. Or, I could create DomainCoin and have it consist of a portfolio of my domains. Or, I could have a DumbCoin, which would be based on the profit share from my Dumb.com website. I could even offer WebsiteCoin to raise money to buy websites, and give a percentage of the monthly profits to the coin holders. The only problem with all of this is that in the USA it is currently illegal, because it violates SEC rules. In June 2014, the SEC charged the owner of SatoshiDICE.com and FeedZeBirds.com with violating securities laws because his "IPOs" were unregistered. The recently passed JOBS Act does make some allowances for crowdfunding (such as if the investors are "accredited" [worth $1 million+ or earn over $200,000+ a year]), and there are also some ways to structure it that may get around SEC regulations like if the investor receives rewards instead of money.

If you are looking to get involved in the cryptocurrency business, you might want to take a look at the forum postings at Bitcointalk.org and read the cryptocurrency news at Bitkoin.com and CoinDesk.com. This will give you a great overview of what is currently happening in the cryptocurrency community.

Why I Am Happy To Sell At A Loss

I sold Weights.com in 2014 for $36,500 and lost money on it. But, I am fine with that. I bought the Weights.com domain name for $32,000 in March of 2012. It currently appraises for $284,000 on Estibot.com (a free automated domain valuation tool), and I think it appraised around that amount back then also. I did not have any grand plans for it, but I figured I could always at least sell it for what I paid. My goal was either to flip the domain for a big profit (I was thinking I might get $100,000 if I found the right buyer), or if that did not work I would create a site on it and make lots of money. Over two years had passed, and both of those objectives were a total failure. I never got any good offers on my own for the domain, and when I tried selling it through domain brokers, all the offers were around the price I paid for it.

I also tried setting up an article-type site on Weights.com, using Wordpress, and paid for 100 custom-written articles about weight lifting and fitness, but the site hardly got any more visitors than when I had the domain parked. It could just be that I am not great at search engine optimization (SEO), which is building your webpages (i.e., choice of key words, design, graphics, etc.) so they get listed well in the search engines. Anyhow, I think the only way to use Weights.com is to build a real site on it, like selling fitness equipment. Or, it could be the home page for a company that sells weights offline (my guess is that weights are not the best product to have to ship).

On the $36,500 sale, I paid a 20% commission (10% to Flippa.com, 5% to the primary broker who handled the Flippa sale for me, and 5% to a co-broker), so my net was only $29,200. That is almost $3,000 less than I paid. I think it was a great deal for the buyer, but I had shopped it around enough to know that it probably wouldn't sell for that much higher. I figured I might as well sell it while I had somebody who wanted to make a deal.

The main point of all this is that once I had done everything I wanted to do with the domain (and failed), it was worth a lot less to me than it was when I first owned it. I am happy I got to try out Weights.com, and I don't regret buying it.

My Paperless Life

Many years ago when I first bought a scanner, I used to tell everyone how great it was to go from a messy stack of papers on my desk to a having paperless office. More recently, I have moved on to even loftier goals. I now try to lead a paperless life. All my business and personal documents exist only in the cloud. I feel a huge sense of freedom, I feel more modern, and I feel more organized. I would liken it to the nirvana of the elusive inbox zero (getting down to 0 unanswered emails in your inbox), or for the less tech overloaded, the feeling of having a clean house/apartment.

Here are the top 10 ways I accomplished my paperless life:

1. **Office Clutter** - I started by converting to a paperless office using a Fujitsu ScanSnap scanner (you can buy one for around $500 on Amazon.com). It converts everything you scan to keyword searchable PDF files. Each pile of papers I had is now a file on my computer. For example, credit card statements from 2014 are 2014CreditCards.pdf. Some files are more general, like 2008-2012BusinessPapers.pdf. The Fujitsu scanner scans both sides of each document, and it is not a problem if the paper sizes vary (e.g., a small receipt). Every few months, I scan in whatever documents I have accumulated, and then at the end of the year I combine them into one big file. As an example, 2014CreditCards1.pdf and 2014CreditCards2.pdf and 2014CreditCards3.pdf all would merge into 2014CreditCards.pdf).

2. **Magazines** - I used to subscribe to many magazines such as *Wired*, *Fast Company*, *Fortune*,

Inc., and *Entrepreneur*, and they would pile up waiting to be read. Now instead I can read those and 140 other magazines (*Rolling Stone, People, US, Time*, etc.) using a service named NextIssue.com, which costs $10-$15/month. For that fixed monthly price, you can read as many of those 140 magazines each month as you want on your mobile phone, tablet, or PC. I read them on my iPhone.

3. **Old Boxes** - I scanned my boxes of childhood memories: old schoolwork, old businesses I had started (I began my entrepreneurial career when I was 10), and old poems I had written. I even scanned my shoebox full of notes from girls, that I had kept all these years. Also, I found some tapes of songs I wrote and recorded as a kid and used a special cord I bought on Amazon.com to transfer the cassettes to MP3 files on my computer.

4. **Music** - No more CDs. I used to have a collection of over 200 CDs, which I eventually copied to MP3 files so I could listen to them on my PC. I then threw out the CDs. A few years ago, I signed up for Rdio.com (unlimited online music for $4.99/month) and have not bought a CD since. They have 99% of all the CDs I owned and 99% of all the new ones I would buy. I recently took it a step further and deleted all my MP3 files from my PC (they were taking up space) since with services like Rdio.com, Spotify.com, Rhapsody, all the old music I like is forever available in the cloud.

5. **Books** - No more books, just e-books. In fact, I have had people give me a book I thought looked great, but I bought the e-book instead of reading the

one they gave me. It is much more convenient for me to read things on my iPhone.

6. **Photos** - I had boxes of old photos, home videos (the old VHS kind), and photo albums from when I was a kid. I shipped them all off to ScanDigital.com, at 70% off via a Groupon offer, where they were converted to digital files. Now I can much more easily share these photos with my family, and they will be better preserved for future generations.

7. **Taxes** - I e-file my income tax returns using TurboTax.com, and all my tax records are scanned into a folder on my PC.

8. **Contracts** - No more printed contracts. I sign contracts online with an e-signature, using services such as HelloSign.com. It is free to use for up to three contracts a month.

9. **Checks** - No more check writing. I make every available effort to use services that offer automated monthly billing or Paypal.

10. **Cloud Storage** - I store all my computer files on a cloud service like DropBox.com (they offer a free plan). That way I can access my files from anywhere on any device. I used to use Gotomypc.com to connect to my office PC, and that worked, but it was slow and not very efficient.

There are also other advantages to being as virtual and paperless as possible. Several times my basement flooded, and things got ruined. Luckily not anything important, but I could have easily lost all of it in a fire or a more severe flood. I have also moved several times, and for every move I had to deal with all my old boxes. And, with everything packed away, I did not have easy access to it. I never knew exactly where certain items were, and a lot of things I just forgot about. Now I have full access to all my stuff, anywhere, anytime, so I highly recommend going paperless.

Some Websites Are Just Not Worth It

Sometimes after I create a site, it turns out to be more trouble than it is worth, so I shut the site down or sell it. Here are some examples:

1. **DigitalCharity.com** - It all started in 2002 when shopaholic Karyn Bosnak asked for donations online to pay off her $20,000 in credit card debt. It worked, and got her huge media attention, and soon people were begging for money for all sorts of things online (college tuition, paying off gambling debts, breast implants, etc.). I created DigitalCharity.com to offer people a free, easy way to do their cyberbegging. They did not need their own website or blog, all they had to do was fill out a form, and their web panhandling plea would be published instantly on my site.

It worked, and lots of people posted heart-wrenching requests for money. I think I even made a few donations myself. But, there were two big problems. First, I received a large number of automated spam submissions, and because I was running custom-built software, there was no easy way to block them, other than manually approving all the submissions. For a site where I was only making $25/month (from banner ads), this was not worth it.

The bigger problem was much more unexpected. Instead of creating a site that helped people in need like I had planned, it turned out some people actually lost money from posting on DigitalCharity.com. What happened was that dozens of scammers trolled the site contacting the cyberbeggars, all people who were desperate for money and would do anything to get it, bombarding them with fake loan offers, advance fee frauds (fake job offers, fake prize notifications, shady business deals, etc.), and every other type of con you can imagine. I know this only because many of the posters to the site would forward these emails to me asking if they were real.

2. **DialPeople.com** - In the mid-2000s when VOIP (Internet phone calls) started to become popular, I created a site where people could use VOIP technology to call a friend or family member. They would type the text they wanted to say into a form on my site and then my server would call the recipient and speak the text (using a computer voice). The call could be anonymous, or you could give your name on the call. It cost me around $800/month in phone call fees, but the site was very popular and was making around $800/month in ad income, so it broke even.

The problems came from people who used the site to do illegal things, like making harassing calls. For example, several times students used my service to call in bomb threats to their schools. I was contacted by the police and FBI several times over incidents like this. I was not in trouble; they just wanted information about whoever made the calls. But getting urgent phone calls from police detectives and FBI agents is not a good thing, and I was worried I could be drawn into a court case or lawsuit.

3. **Confessions.net** - I started the site in the mid-2000s by buying a database of 4,000 confessions from another confessions site that went out of business. I then collected 20,000+ additional confessions through user submissions after I launched the site, and the site became very popular, but there were problems:

A) Some of the confessions were obviously fake. They just sounded stupid, silly, or made no sense.

B) The site got hacked several times and was constantly being targeted by autoposting spam bots.
C) Many of the confessions were about illegal events.
D) Some of the confessions listed actual names or other identifying information, or slandered people.

I frequently received angry emails from people wanting certain listings removed, and they threatened to call the police and sue me if I did not do it immediately. I always complied with their requests, but other times I was contacted by the police, lawyers/prosecutors, or FBI agents looking for information about particular postings. I was even subpoenaed several times.

Considering I only made around $10/month from the site (as I could not run ads from major ad networks due to the offensive/r-rated content), all of this was not worth it. Eventually I stopped taking confession submissions and deleted all the confessions from the site other than a handful of clean ones that will not cause problems. I then picked out a few hundred clean ones and used them to build a confessions section on my Dumb.com website.

4. **Ever want to start a site to host free web pages or images? Don't.**

I bought several image hosting sites, but I eventually ended up selling them for less than I paid. It was a huge hassle to run them. I was constantly having hacking and server overload problems, and I needed to pay workers in India to constantly delete all the r-rated images. Uploads of copyrighted images were also a huge problem. Because of that, it was too risky to run Google ads on this type of site. I did run them on the main page and the image upload form page, but that did make a lot of money since the picture pages were the ones that got the most page views.

Bandwidth usage was another big issue. I had one of my sites spread over nine dedicated Linux servers, and that worked well, but there would be spikes where it was doing way over my web host's bandwidth quota. If I limited the bandwidth to the 10 Mbps each server allowed, then the site would slow to a crawl because of bandwidth throttling. Nowadays there is more sophisticated technology that can handle this, and bandwidth is cheaper and less of a problem, but I think it is still hard to get decent ad revenue from an image hosting site. It is a good project for somebody who has a lot of time to deal with the ad sales and all the site problems, but not something I am interested in doing anymore.

Over the years, I have bought several free web hosting sites, where users can create and host their own websites at no cost. It was initially appealing to think I can put ads on all the sites that webmasters created, but in the end it was not worth it. There were constant server problems due to programs/databases the webmasters would run, and there were also many hacking-related problems. Plus, I would sometimes get complaints about the content of various pages. The ads on the sites were very low paying and there was never a month when I made money from owning a free web hosting site. In the end, I either sold or shut down all the free web hosting sites that I bought.

A few years ago, one of my business associates bought a free web hosting site (even though I told him not to) and he sold it at a big loss after a month. The problem was that at the time he bought it, it was making $1,000/month profit from affiliate commissions from webmasters who upgraded to paid hosting plans. But, it turns out the web hosting affiliate program had a much lower payout to free web hosting sites, and once they found out that was the type of site he owned, they cut his payout by 90% and he started losing money.

Buying Cheap Traffic

In more recent years, the new sites I create get minimal traffic. This is frustrating, disappointing, and not good business, and I am not sure exactly what to do about it. In the olden days, it used to be if you built a good site, people would find it. Google would send it lots of traffic, other sites would link to it; it was one big traffic party. I never advertised, I never did link trades, I hardly did any SEO, and no social media promotion.

Things have changed, and I am lost in a sea littered with my own dead sites. I have tried using Facebook and Twitter, but for me that has never resulted in extra visitors (yes, I know everybody else in the world seems to just magically add a Share button to their site and the world comes running to their door). I have tried advertising (like on AdSense), but I never once have made more money than I spent. I have tried buying links on sites, but Google now frowns on that, plus I am not sure that was ever worth it anyway. I have paid people to do white hat SEO (Google likes this) and black hat SEO (Google does not like this), but none of it worked. ("White hat SEO" is the process of trying to get your site listed higher in the search engines using strategies that follow the rules and focus on areas such as keywords, link building, and creating relevant content. "Black hat SEO" refers to gaming the system by targeting the automated methods search engines use to rank sites, and is against the rules). The few sites I have right now that are listed #1 in Google all used my special "No SEO" method. I just create a good site, do nothing extra to get listed higher, and Google shows me some much-needed love. The point is you don't necessarily have to do any SEO to get listed at the top of the search engines.

The vast majority of the time, my sites live in cyber wasteland, dying a slow death like a great painting hidden in an attic or a moving poem kept locked in a diary but never shared. My sites want to break free. They want to be seen and heard. They yearn to be liked, to be commented on, to be shared. Yet, day after day I sit idly by and do nothing. I am the problem, and I am the solution.

So, I finally got off my ass to do something about it. I designed what I called "The Great Traffic Experiment of 2015." The subject of my experiment was my recently launched site at GameReviews.com, which was getting around 20 visitors per day. I had done nothing to promote it. My hypothesis was that if I bought traffic for the site, Google would somehow see lots of people are going to it (Google knows all, sees all), and rank it higher. I also thought maybe some of the people going to the site would keep coming back even after I stopped advertising. To keep things as scientific as possible, I determined that the best course of action would be to buy traffic from one source at a time. I then would see if it was getting more traffic than before the ad started. That way I could determine how good that particular source of traffic was. If I did not get any repeat traffic, it was not worth buying again.

That all sounds good, but I am an impatient type of guy, so I threw that protocol out the window, typed *cheap traffic* into Google, and within minutes bought visitors from 5 different sources of cheap traffic all at once: Gamesbanner-net.com, Easyvisitors.com, Maxvisits.com, Cpmoz.com and Hitscheap.com. Some of the traffic was from video game sites, but most wasn't. Some was from pop-unders, some was in the form of 404 error page redirect traffic, and the rest came from unknown sources. Most was from the USA. The cost was ranged from $1-$10 per 1,000 visitors, but mostly around $1 for 1,000 visitors (this experiment was all about cheap, low-quality traffic).

My Google Analytics reports for GameReviews.com showed useful stats for each traffic source, such as how many pages each visitor went to (if they only went to the main page of the site but not subpages, they probably were not that interested), how long they stayed on the site (if they left the site quickly, they were not too interested), and the bounce rate (how many people left the site right away without really looking at it). This let me compare sources, to see which gave me the best traffic. The only problem was that many of these cheap traffic sources send the traffic in frames or other ways that can distort the stats. For example, when GameReviews.com opens as a pop-under ad, I assume that makes it look like the user stayed on the site a long time, but it may just be they never bothered to close the pop-under window or even look at my site.

One result, as I expected, was that the cheap traffic was not nearly as valuable as people who go to my site directly (like by typing GameReviews.com into their browser or from searching in Google). Those high-quality users look at around 2.2 pages each and stay on the site for 2.5 minutes. The cheap traffic usually stayed on the site less than 10 seconds and visited less than 1.3 pages per session. The video game site traffic from Gamesbannernet.com did better than all the other cheap traffic, but cost 5-10 times more, so I am not sure if it was worth it.

All that really mattered was how much traffic I kept getting after all the ads were done. Overall, I spent $100 for approximately 25,000 visitors, and it did not lead to any repeat traffic or search engine traffic. I still just get the 20 visitors a day, like I did before.

How I Was Scammed Out of $2,000

In my 15+ years of doing business online, I have lost money to scammers several times. I thought I would show an example of one particular scam I fell for, as a warning for other webmasters who might be in a similar situation. What makes it unusual is that eventually I was able to get an admission of guilt from the scammer. Here's what happened:

Five years ago, I decided to set up mini-sites (small, content based sites) on 4,000 of my unused domain names. Because Google frowns on having duplicate content on sites, I decided to make it so each of my mini-sites had mostly unique content. I could have paid article writers to write articles for each of my domains one by one (like on GetMortgages.com, for example, they would write mortgage-related articles), but because I have domains that cover almost any topic, it was a lot cheaper and faster to just buy pre-written articles in bulk from dozens of different writers. Many article writers have a big backlog of unsold articles, and some also have articles that they have written for other customers but never got paid for. It is usually very hard for anybody to sell articles like these in bulk because most webmasters only want very specific types of articles for whatever site they are building, so I was able to buy these articles at less than half the usual prices (most articles sell for two cents per word).

Over several months, I bought 14,000 articles from dozens of different writers. The problem was that I either had to trust the article writer by prepaying them, or they had to send me the articles ahead of time and trust that I would pay. This worked out fine for most of my transactions, but the article writing business is notorious for fraud. Many writers sell articles as "unique" even though they have already sold them to other clients (this makes the articles almost worthless), or they sell articles as unique that were actually copied from other sites (these are also worthless). Or, they sell articles as unique but they are really automated article rewrites (there the output of an article spinner program, which takes an original article and then changes the words by using synonyms and changing the order of the words). There are also some writers who ask for prepayment, and then for one reason or another never get the work done.

I had all these types of problems on a small scale with various writers, but overall I was happy with the articles I purchased, and over time I learned how to avoid getting ripped off. But, there was one writer that scammed me out of $2,000, and I am still angry about it. What it came down to was that I was busy that day and in a rush and made a critical mistake. I will get to that in a minute though. Here is what transpired:

I made a deal with Navendra Pillai (email: naven114@gmail.com) to buy $2,000 worth of articles (at $1 per article) that he had written already but had not sold. He convinced me to prepay him, which I did, but he never sent me any of the articles. Normally I would just dispute the charge with Paypal.com and try to get my money back, but the critical mistake I made was that I was out of my office when he sent me the request for the $2,000, so I paid using the Paypal app on my Blackberry. What I did not realize was that all payments made that way went through as personal payments, not as business payments (even though the app used my business Paypal account), and there was no way to request a refund from Payal for personal payments. So, I was screwed.

A few months later, Navendra Pillai tried to sell me more articles using a different name and email address (Ganesha Pillai - visionzzolution@gmail.com). By then, I had dealt with so many article writers I did not recognize that he had the same last name. Luckily, after going back and forth with him a few times, I got suspicious. I did some checking and found a forum posting talking about how visionzzolution@gmail.com is really Navendra Pillai and how he defrauded a bunch of people. When I confronted him with this info, he wrote: "I'm sorry you are talking to the wrong guy here my name is Vinod ganesha Pillai.. If you're not interested just please tell ur not interested.. Will look elsewhere to sell those articles...don't determine another person because you were fooled before. Thanks and regards. Nice doing job with ya.."

After I sent him a few more emails (I kept the conversation going by pretending I might buy some new articles from him if he first delivered the ones he owed me), he finally gave in and admitted his guilt. He wrote: "I'm really sorry to scam you... And others i did not scam them is just that sometimes they work as writers for me and the clients dun pay so i couldn't pay.. Thats the matter. In your case i supposed to send the articles and than somethings happened and it made be to be a scammer.. Will make sure such incidents wont happen again. Sorry and thanks for asking for articles from me again.."

The next day he wrote: "Well i would like to tell you this, I got to know about freelance writing thing and all at the age of 18 and i recruited certain reliable writers and started our work as a team of writers and wrote lots of articles for clients and websites. The work was going on all and after sometime certain clients so called clients made bulk orders and so on so we worked on it and they suddenly disappeared with the articles. And i was the one to be blamed and i took all the responsibilities and i paid some of them from my own pocket and i lost lots of money because few writers threatened to lodge police report against me and certain writers understood my situation. Thats why you can see lots of people posted that i'm a scammer and so on. If anyone in my position also would have done so. I'm not a very rich guy either studying somemore. Can' be expecting my parents for all my studies expanses and so on. I was a scholarship student doing my Chemical Engineering Degree. And my scholarship was ripped off because i didnt do one of my semester well. It was all because of the clients scammed and the things i got from my writers. I even do not know whether the writers have sold my articles not.. Maybe they would have sold them as PLR articles too i'm not sure. Thats why i'm not confident at all that the articles may pass copyscape. Moreover, because i was mad at a client who scammed me more than $10,000 where he promised and never kept the promise and just disappeared. Than that time i got to know you and you requested articles from me from my previous email. I thought i want to be honest and provide all the articles to you. But the hatred against the client made me to scam you.. I am in regret doing such thing to you. But this time i really wanted to do business with you and clear all the articles. But like what everyone says you can never run away from the mischiefs you do. I agree with that. Even i gave my mothers particular and her account because i want the money to go to her. Let's say the articles don't pass copyscape and the have been used by others i know it is fair for me not to be paid. But, i'm really in a bad situation that i am in need of money i'm ready to do anything for you and even ready to work for you for years if only you can give me $3000 to $4000. I will really appreciate your help friend. i am ready to do any task for you. Please do help me. I have a big faith and believe in you. Just if i manage to finish my course i can pay the amount borrowed within months. I am to finish my studies next year begining friend. I am really looking forward for your help. I know you came up in your life with hardwork and so on. I would like to take you as my role model and start working harder with your guidelines if you're to help me friend. SO really looking forward to your help."

I did not do any more business with him, but I was at least happy I got him to admit his mistakes. Also, in case it helps potential future scam victims identify him, he emailed me his wire payment info:

MALAYAN BANKING BERHAD
NAME : MAHESWARI D/O RASANGAM
City: KLANG
Swift Code: MBBEMYKL
Account Number: 112455313678

When he emailed me this wire info, he wrote "..this account belongs to my mother. So i can never scam friend."

When you run hundreds of sites, bad situations like this are just the cost of doing business. Each time, I learn from it, and in the future try not to make the same mistakes again.

To help other people avoid getting scammed when paying for goods or services online, I offer the following tips:

1. Always Google the person (or company) you are dealing with. Google their name, and then separately Google their email address, and see what comes up. Also, put quotes around their name, so Google only shows results matching that exact name. If there are a lot of results, try Googling their

name or email with the word scam after it like: "Navendra Pillai" scam

2. Be very wary of prepaying somebody by wiring them or using Western Union, because there is no way to ever get it back.

3. Most people will tell you that if you pay by Paypal there is no risk because you can just dispute the charge (like with a credit card), but they are misinformed. I have initiated dozens of Paypal disputes and, assuming you are disputing a transaction for virtual/intangible goods (not something that is physically shipped) or a service, it is almost impossible to win. It does not matter if it was a total scam or you are just not happy with the quality of what you received. The only time I have won a dispute like that was when the seller did not respond at all (or maybe instead they approved the refund when Paypal emailed them that I was disputing it).

4. Refuse to pay anything up front. If needed, give partial payments as the work progresses. For example, if it is a $2,000 project, pay them $100 immediately after they do the first $100 worth of work, and then keep making payments as they do more work.

5. When possible, use an escrow service, such as Escrow.com. This greatly reduces the risk for both the buyer and the seller.

Striking It Rich With Bitcoin Cloud Mining

Once you start hearing too much about Bitcoin, you probably start to zone out, so instead of boring you with additional examples of how Bitcoin works and new ways it can be used, I will dazzle you with a look at a more interesting, more understandable, and more exciting part of the cryptocurrency world: Bitcoin Mining.

Reminiscent of the California Gold Rush of the 1850s, there is currently a frenzy to get into the mining of cryptocurrencies. Unlike traditional ("fiat") currencies such as US Dollars, which are printed by the government, most cryptocoins are mined by the general public. Just like with prospecting for gold, diamonds, and oil, you need to buy the equipment, find a location, have the technical knowledge to get everything set up, and then keep everything running long enough to at least make back your original investment.

All this reminds me a little of when I used to hunt for expired domain names in the 1990s. There was no automated software for it, so I spent hours a day searching for unregistered domains by hand. Each time I would find a good one and grab it; I felt like I struck gold.

As with domain names, cryptocoins are mined using computers. You basically turn your PC processing time and power into money by running mining software that "digs" for cryptocurrency using math. It is similar to how when years ago large companies and universities used to rent people small blocks of time on their supercomputers (for complex math, medical research, architecture, cryptography, weather modeling, etc.), that computing time had a value. Now you can unlock value in any computer by turning computing time into cryptocoins, even just using your regular home PC (most people buy specialized PCs though, known as "mining rigs," which are optimized for mining).

The problem is that if it were that easy to get rich from Bitcoin mining, everyone would be doing it. The revenue the average Bitcoin miner gets is constantly adjusted so it is only slightly more than the costs involved. More importantly, much like with mining for gold, the path to Bitcoin riches is paved with problems (if you have ever watched TV reality shows like *Gold Rush*, *Jungle Gold*, *Ice Cold Gold*, *Bering Sea Gold*, or even *Deadliest Catch*, you know the kind of things that can happen). The list below is just some of what you have to deal with:

- Complex set up and installation.

- Large electricity consumption - Unlike a normal PC which stands idle much of the time, or has low CPU usage programs, mining runs 24/7 and completely maxes out the processors of the PC at all times.

- Internet connectivity issues - If your Internet goes down, your business is dead in the water.

- Computer space and cooling problems (mining PCs run very hot).

- The prices of cryptocurrencies fluctuate wildly, so even if everything goes well, if the price of bitcoin goes down by 50% after the first few months of mining, you will lose money.

- Annoying noise (the cooling fans run non-stop and get loud).

- Hardware failures - Because the PC runs constantly, things tend to break.

- Security - The cryptocurrency business is full of hackers and resides in the Wild Wild West of the Internet.

- Scams - The only way to stay ahead of the competition is to pre-order new, more powerful mining rigs, but many times the companies selling them are fraudulent, and you lose your investment.

- Even once you have everything set up and working perfectly, you constantly need to upgrade your equipment, and the problems start all over again.

One way around many of these problems is to rent servers for cryptocoin mining, just like most website owners rent servers for hosting their sites. For example, this can be done cheaply using Amazon's Elastic Compute Cloud (EC2) platform. But, it is hard to make it profitable, and you still need to be a programmer type to handle the complex set up involved. Using a low priced VPS (such as DigitalOcean.com for $5/month) is another option, but that is generally not profitable either. A Harvard student unsuccessfully tried an even lower cost solution, before he was banned from the university's computer labs for using the school's supercomputer for cryptocurrency mining.

Some other, more unusual, ways to mine cryptocurrencies include:

Solar Powered Server Farms - Electricity is one of the biggest costs in Bitcoin mining, so using solar power can greatly reduce the costs.

Bitcoin Mining In Space - A solar powered mining rig in space is closer to the sun and would get sunlight 24/7.

Oil Immersion Cooling – Uses approximately 1/3 less power, mostly from the cooling fans being removed from the PCs. This greatly reduces the mining cost.

Quantum Powered Computers – Several companies are already working on building computers powered by quantum mechanics (throw out everything you think you know about how atoms work, and strap yourself in for a wild ride in this crazy area of physics). These would be much faster than normal PCs, and use much less electricity, resulting in higher Bitcoin mining profits. It could be decades before this technology is ready though.

The most appealing new option for the average user is cloud Bitcoin mining. It saves you from having to deal with installation, setup, and all the other hassles and risks of running a Bitcoin mining company. Instead, your mining operation happens in "the cloud," which means a hosting type company handles everything for you and you just need to log in to your online account and see how much money you are making. It sounds good, but does it live up to the hype?

In the Summer of 2014, I decided to give cloud mining a try. I had never done any regular Bitcoin mining, but I had read enough about it to know generally how it worked. After a quick Google search, I set up accounts with these 3 cryptocoin cloud mining companies [unless you are interested in the boring technical details, skip to the results section]:

1. **The Hashlet from GAW Miners** - For mining Bitcoin and Scrypt-based altcoins. Lets you choose from various mining pools. I bought 1 Hashlet for $15.99. There was a maintenance fee of $.08/day for each 1 MH. Payouts were once every 24 hours. The mining was to continue as long as your Hashlet

makes a profit (mining income - maintenance fees). This makes it hard to estimate a return on investment, but it is better than having a fixed length contract. Also, another thing to keep in mind, is that with all mining, the profitability of existing mining equipment goes down over time because the way Bitcoin is designed, the mathematical difficulty of mining increases periodically to keep up with advances in technology. The result of this is that older machines make less money, unless the part of your cloud mining contract is that they automatically upgrade.

2. **Cex.io** - You buy computing power ("hashing power") in the form of the "ghash" (GHS), which is a cryptocoin that represents virtual mining power (1 GHS coin = 1 GH/s hashrate). Cex.io deducts a maintenance fee of 18 cents per month per GH and then automatically pays out your Bitcoin (or you can choose to mine other cryptocoins) via there zero fee mining pool at ghash.io. I spent $4.75 (it was really $5, but I had to pay a transaction fee to site where I was storing my Bitcoins) to buy 2.5 GH. Payouts are usually every hour or two. This mining contract pays out as long as you hold it (a unique feature is that you can sell it if you want, via the sale of your GHS coins). So, it is more like owning a stock (the GHS coin) that pays dividends (your cloud mining earnings). If the price of the GHS coin does not go down, you are guaranteed at least to get back your initial investment. So, any cloud mining earnings you get are a bonus.

3. **CloudHashers** - I paid $9.95 for one 24-Hour Scrypt Mining Contract (Litecoin, Dogecoin, etc.), which has an advertised hash rate of 1MH/s.

Payouts were every one to two hours. I had to first sign up with a mining pool, because the CloudHashers payouts go to your mining pool, so I joined Wemineltc.com. What confuses me, though, is that I received payouts for three days, even though I bought a 24-hour contract.

Results: It was not worth it. GAW Miners and CloudHashers both went out of business within a year, and Cex.io has put their cloud mining service on hold because it was not profitable. While they were working, all three services did make mining payouts to me, but none were enough to cover what I invested. I am pretty sure I would also have lost money if I had bought my own mining equipment (computers), so at least this was an easier way to lose money.

My First Kiss

In a previous chapter, I talked about my First Date in middle school. We fell in love, but never kissed. I wanted to of course, but we were young and inexperienced, and it never ended up happening.

Then came high school. I did not have any wild romances, but some days I would walk a girl named Heather home from school. We would hang out at her house. Sometimes we would be alone in her room. We were not dating, but I am sure she knew I liked her. One time we were on her bed, and she closed her eyes and just lay there. I was pretty sure she wanted me to kiss her, but I was an awkward teenage boy, and a small amount of doubt in my mind along with a big lack of courage kept me from doing it. Then a few months later we were on her bed again, and she closed her eyes, and I said "what the hell" (silently, in my head of course) and went in for the kiss. It was great (it was not her first kiss, so from her point of view I am sure I was not very good), and I was on cloud nine. We were never a couple but were together like that a few more times over the next year. I always will have fond memories of my days with her. But, I regret how shy I was. I regret how much of a dork I was. I regret not taking charge more; I regret thinking too much and not being free enough.

Why is it in the business world, I have no fear? Even before the Internet came along, as a kid, I was an entrepreneur. Always thinking about money, always scheming to get rich, going to auctions/flea markets/tag sales, doing business deals with adults, and generally acting like a little business tycoon. Then I grew up, hopped on the information superhighway, and was soon buying flower stores I had never seen, inventing toys, conquering the domain name market, and doing multi-million dollar deals.

I am trying to increase my confidence in my personal life to equal that of my business endeavors. Maybe it was stupid, maybe I am just a wimp, but recently I climbed up on the roof of my house. I know, "no big deal," you say. Well, it was for me. I am not scared of heights, but I don't usually take physical risks. I don't want to get hurt. A guy was at my house this winter clearing the ice off my roof and was telling me about how while he was up there he noticed the chimney flashing was messed up and should be fixed. He told me I should go up and take a look, and I said "No need, I believe you, go ahead and do the work." A few days later he came back and again, he and the guy who works for him both were telling me I should take a look myself. I really didn't care at this point, but they keep asking me to go up there, almost like peer pressure chanting "Do It, Do It," and I was so ready to say my usual "No" when it occurred to me that I should try doing the opposite of what I usually do, and it was an opportunity to do something exciting. In a split second I blurted out "OK." Now, the week before I had just had a conversation with the wife of a neurosurgeon who said that her husband was treating an unusually large number of men that were falling of roofs while trying to scrape off snow and ice due to the record winter in this part of the country. This was in the back of my mind the whole time. I was also thinking about my wife and kids and how I might make one wrong step and fall and die, and that would be very stupid. It actually turned out to be just as scary and dangerous as I thought it would be, but I did it and lived to tell the tale. I am not sure what lesson I learned from this.

I think what it all comes down to is that I always have known a lot about the business world. It is where I feel comfortable. Now, as a middle-aged adult, I think I also have a good handle on many of the things in life. But, even after 46 years, I still don't know much about girls.

Giving Away My New Business Ideas

I have decided to share some of my new business ideas. I am not currently working on any of these, but would if I had more time [the domains listed below are just examples of domains I used to own]:

1. **RunWebsites.com** - A service that manages websites for Internet companies 24 hours a day, 7 days a week, similar to how a real estate management company manages rental properties for the building owner. This would be a combination of being a webmaster, a programmer, customer service, a server admin, and website monitoring. I can hire an employee to run sites for me, but they are not available nights and weekend, plus they usually can't do everything. Programmers usually are not proficient at running sites, and people who run sites are usually not able to do programming or fix server problems. I have used low-cost companies in India for many of these tasks, but somebody still needs to be in charge and manage the company in India, so that is not a full-service solution. If I did not have to spend so much time managing my sites, I would create a lot more of them, and also buy more of them.

2. **FindKids.com** - A website where you upload a photo of your missing/abducted child, and it searches photos online for matches (using an age-progressed version of your photo). Sometimes the child is living in a new location under a new name, but still appears in school photos or social networking profiles. Yes, it is a long shot that there

will be a match, but if you are a desperate parent it is worth trying anything that has even a small chance of finding your child.

3. **DetectLies.com** - A lie detector website where you give a friend/lover/spouse a lie detector test by having them talk into a microphone on their computer. You enter the questions ahead of time into the website, and email the person a link to the test. It will then show you the results.

4. **SeeingEyeHumans.com** - A paid mobile phone app for blind people which they would use when they need help with something. For a short period they would use their phone to stream video of what they are looking at and the "Seeing Eye Human" (a low-cost worker in India or Africa or Russia) would describe it to them over the phone. I don't know anybody who is blind, so I have no idea what blind people specifically need help with, but I think this would be good for them to have for emergencies (like if they are lost) or even just things like finding the right cereal at the supermarket or if they are going on a date and want to know if they look OK.

5. **FunTimelines.com** - A site like Dipity.com where you can create your own timelines, but with a twist. Instead of just being able to create the usual historical type timeline, users could create alternate fantasy timelines showing what would have happened if things had been different, like if Michael Jackson had not died, or if the US lost World War II. Kind of like a fan fiction site, but using timelines instead of stories.

6. **WebHaters.com** (or maybe NotFriends.com) - A Facebook social network type site, but linking to-

gether people who have in common people or companies that they hate.

7. **CrazyImpressions.com** - Create a site where people submit YouTube-type videos of their celebrity impressions.

8. **RaiseCash.com** - As we saw from the banking crisis of 2008, giving out loans is a risky business. But, there are a lot of desperate people who would pay high interest rates to get personal loans (no collateral), so they don't get evicted from their apartment or lose their house, or maybe to fund a business. The problem is that states have usury laws that prevent lenders from charging high enough interest rates to compensate them for the big risk involved. Also, people desperate for money usually have trouble making the monthly payments. My solution would be to give people a long-term loan without them having to make any payments until they get back on their feet. It would be more like an investment in the person, a kind of venture capital for people instead of businesses, where I would get a percentage of their future income as repayment for the loan. This is similar to a sports agent type contract, where the agent gets part of everything the player makes.

9. **BoneoftheMonth.com** - I registered the domain in 2003 and the concept was to create a site where people could buy their pet a luxurious gift, which would be a gourmet dog bone delivered by mail to them each month for a year. Each month a different type of bone would be mailed to the dog. In addition to pet owners buying this gift for their pet, it would also be a great holiday gift for friends and family to

give to the owner/pet. The good thing about the dog bone business is that bones are cheap to buy and are easy to purchase. Just to get started, I could buy them from a local pet store at the retail price, and not have to worry about setting up a wholesale account or carrying much inventory. The scheduled shipping could be automated using Fulfillment By Amazon and the website part would be simple since there would only be one main item for sale (a one-year club membership). I would have the user choose small, medium, or large sized bones, depending on the size of their dog. The problem is that I just don't think there is enough profit to be made from it, but maybe you can figure out a way for it to work. The bones only cost a few dollars each, but the shipping each month would cost $5-$10 (some bones are heavy). For example, if the combined cost of the bone and shipping is $10, that means my wholesale cost for a one-year membership would be $120 (12 months x $10 each month). Then there are the labor costs of preparing and mailing each order, and the e-commerce costs (at least 5% for merchant fees and fraud). On top of all of that, there is the cost of obtaining customers, such as by advertising in Google. The ad cost would probably be at least $10 per order, making my total costs around $150 per order. I can't imagine people would pay more than $99, or even $49, for a gift like this for a pet, so I never launched the site. Maybe if I sold a three-month plan (or a quarterly one) instead it could be at a price people would pay, but having it only for three months does not sound like a very exciting product. Every Christmas when I see all the various gift products advertised, the BoneoftheMonth.com idea pops back into my head, but for now it is not something I am going to pursue.

10. **Escrow Ideas** - I had three new business ideas recently, all related to escrow services:

A) Kickstarter Escrow - The biggest complaint about crowdfunding sites like Kickstarter.com and Indiegogo.com is that many times people put up their hard-earned money to pre-order a new product, but the item never gets manufactured and delivered. There is almost no accountability at all on these types of sites, so if they want to, the person or company raising the money can pretty much just walk away from the deal and keep the money without delivering the product they advertised. Either it starts out as fraud by a person who is just out to scam the public, or delay after delay causes the buyer to wish they had never invested. Examples of this include the Confederate Express video game, which made national news because the owners of the company developing it are alleged Airbnb squatters, so their Kickstarter campaigns are now in doubt also. Other well-known problem Kickstarter projects include Healbe, Ritot, TellSpec, and Kobe Red, and there is even a site at KickScammed.com dedicated to exposing Kickstarter fraud.

A possible solution to this would be for an escrow type company to hold the crowdfunded money in escrow and pay it directly to the suppliers, similar to how a construction loan is handled in real estate. This would not guarantee the product would get launched, because the company could still fail, but at least it would eliminate people who raise money in bad faith and never plan to deliver the product.

Or, all the crowdfunded money could be put in escrow until the product actually starts shipping, and instead you loan money to a company based on all the pre-orders (and guaranteed payments) they received via the crowdfunding site, plus maybe some other collateral. If the product never gets delivered, the buyers would get all their money back (from being held in escrow), and the escrow/finance company would take the loss.

It would greatly benefit a Kickstarter.com-type product to use escrow because it would get a much higher response rate for fundraising due to investors not having to worry as much about losing their investment.

B) E-Book Escrow - In a 2014 TechCrunch.com article *How To Save Books* by Jon Evans, he proposed a business model where readers pay nothing for e-books up front, and instead pay only after they read them (basically, they only pay for books they liked). In a comment to this article, Jeremy Lee James suggested that the reader could "buy" the e-book from Amazon.com by depositing the purchase price into an escrow type account controlled by Amazon, and then download the e-book. The author would only receive the payment from Amazon if the reader gets to the end of the book (Amazon already automatically monitors what pages the reader has read). If the book is not finished after a certain length of time, it would be deleted from their e-reader, and their money would be returned to them.

I am not sure if Amazon will ever do this, but it would not be hard to set up a 3rd party escrow service for this purpose, that self-publishing authors could use to sell their e-books. Or, you could set up your own e-bookstore site with built-in escrow, and sign up authors sell their books in it.

C) Bitcoin Escrow - Unlike when paying with a credit card or by Paypal, there is no way to dispute a Bitcoin (or any other type of cryptocurrency) transaction. So, if you pay somebody $100 in Bitcoin online for a used Xbox and they never send it to you; there is almost nothing you can do about it. There are several Bitcoin escrow services you can use to protect yourself such as BTCrow.com but all of these are relatively new sites, and none are established escrow services, like how Escrow.com is the leader for domain escrow. If a more well-known service started offering escrow for Bitcoin transactions, they might be able to obtain significant market share. The problem with anything cryptocurrency related is that there is a lot of fraud and very little trust, so people have no reason to trust these smaller escrow services since they don't have much of a history.

There Is Nothing New Anymore

I bought a new computer recently. It was a top of the line PC for $1,100. But, it really is no better than the last high-level computer I bought in 2009. In fact, it is worse because it has Windows 8. Other than the interface change, I don't think I would notice the difference if I used both computers side by side. This is a significant shift from previous decades, when every few years I would buy a new computer, and it would be a huge change in my life. The new computer would be 2-3 times more powerful, 2-3 times faster, have vastly more hard drive space, and have other handy new features (like built-in wireless, USB ports, DVD writer, etc.). I would feel refreshed, ready to conquer the Internet, at least for another few years until my new computer became out of date.

Same thing with cell phones. Five years ago I switched from a Blackberry to an iPhone. A whole new world opened up for me, and it totally changed where and when I could do business. More recently I went from the iPhone 4 to the iPhone 5, and it was a big nothing. Then there is the iPhone 6, which I care even less about. It used to be that at least new technology was always smaller even if it was not better, but now I am supposed to upgrade just to make my phone bigger?

Domains are another area where there is nothing new. Over 15 years ago, the .com world was in a frenzy when various country domains like nu., .ws, and .cc became available to anyone. Then in the 2000s, the same thing happened when domains such as .biz, .co, and .mobi were launched. Yes, it may be different this time, and even a game changer, with the thousands of new domain extensions currently being introduced, but it is still really just the same old scenario played out on a larger scale.

For the past few years, everybody has been all aflutter about "the cloud." It is really just a more modern, user-friendly term for the Internet. The cloud is great, and I love using it, but with a little work all of this was able to be accomplished back in the 1990s (I know, because I used to do it). You could always put photos, videos, or software on servers. You could always have flexible capacity when hosting a site (using load balancers, for example). The cloud just makes it much more convenient and much, much cheaper. The cloud is not so much a use of new of technology, but a reflection of the huge decrease in server-related costs, the widespread availability of high-speed Internet service, and the paradigm shift towards mobile devices.

Even Bitcoin is not something totally new. Digital currencies (such as E-gold) have been around since the 1990s. Bitcoin is a gigantic step forward in both the technology and the move towards mass adoption. It really is something useful and innovative. The downside is that there are too many problems with it right now. Mt. Gox went bankrupt almost crashing the entire market, leaving thousands of customers penniless (bitcoinless?). More recently, another leading exchange named Bitstamp had around $5 million stolen from it, and had to temporarily shut down (it is back up now). More recently, Bitcoin payment processor EgoPay shut down amid rumors that founders of the company may have stolen millions in funds from clients. This is all in addition to the hundreds of low-level cryptocurrency scams and illegal cryptocurrency sites. Cryptocurrencies are the Wild West of the Internet, filled with hackers, thieves, and cyber dangers. There's gold in dem der hills, but finding it is not a risk that most people want to take until things settle down.

Drones? I used to fly remote-controlled airplanes and helicopters when I was a kid 40 years ago. Now they just scotch tape a camera to it. Plus, almost all the good stuff that can be done with drones violates FAA rules. Amazon and others are working on getting this changed, but until then it is all a big headache.

Virtual reality is cool, although not really something new. In the early 1990s, Sega made a VR headset for arcade games. In 1992, Computer Gaming World magazine predicted "Affordable VR by 1994," and it was a hot topic in movies (*Tron*, *Lawnmower Man*, etc.). Now in 2015, Google Glass is $1,500, and it is not really VR in the classic sense (it is more "augmented reality"). The public can't even buy Google Glass (only developers can). The Oculus Rift VR device looks great, but you can't buy that yet either. Once it launches, it may be something truly amazing. I want one. It won't come out until 2016 though. Magic Leap is also working on an amazing VR device that changes how you see the world around you, but it could be years until that comes out.

When the Internet entered the scene in 1994-1995, that was an exciting time. When the Blackberry and iPhone (or even the iPod) were invented, that was an exciting time. I am sure my parents would say when they first bought a TV or Microwave or VCR they felt the same way. When I bought my first TiVo DVR in 1999, that was exciting. When I watched a music video online for the first time in 1997, that was exciting. I want more of that. I want my technology hunger to be fed. I want to be shocked and surprised. I want to see an ad for something and feel compelled to run to the store to buy it (OK, I will just open a new browser window to Amazon.com and have it overnight shipped to me). I am dying in a wasteland of rehashed ideas and new and improved things that really aren't. Stimulate my brain. Lighten my wallet. Give me something new to play with.

Mistakes and Failures

It is helpful to learn from other peoples' mistakes, so in that spirit, here is a list of some business mistakes I have made that I did not already talk about in this book:

- **Get-Rich-Quick Schemes** - Before the Internet came along, I spent several years buying "no money down" real estate. It was like the current "flipping houses" fad, but back then mortgage companies had much looser rules and it was possible to use some creative techniques to buy an investment property no money down. It was great experience for me, but being a landlord was a lot of headaches, and because I had no money, any time something went wrong (like a roof leak) I had to fix it the cheapest way possible. This would inevitably lead to more problems. Because I was broke, the only way I could get into real estate was with no money down. I don't regret it, but it was a lot of work and risk for very little profits. My downfall came when a tenant accidentally caused a fire in an 8-unit building I owned, resulting in significant damage. I received a $30,000 insurance check, but that only covered the hypothetical cost of repairs. The building department mandated I had to bring it up to code, in order to make the 100-year-old building habitable again, in addition to repairing it. This meant, among other things, that it needed all new plumbing and electrical. This was going to cost $100,000. I used the insurance money to make some repairs, but it was not fast enough for the building inspector, who considered the site a safety hazard, so the city eventually demolished it. Unfortunately, I still had a $50,000 mortgage, and I still had to pay taxes every year on the now vacant land. Plus, the city added a lien for the costs of demolishing it. I called the mortgage company and told them they now had a mortgage on a house that was no longer there, but that instead of defaulting on the loan, I just wanted them to change it to 0% interest. They eventually agreed to that. Many years later I was able to pay off the mortgage and give the land to the city for free in exchange for the cancelation of the lien. Aside from real estate, I also tried other risky money-making ventures, such as owning a 976 pay-per-call number, network marketing (MLM), and investing in penny stocks. None of those ever made any money either.

- **Buying Websites** - I lost money on almost every site I ever purchased. For example, I bought two entertainment websites in 2012 for around $80,000. For the first one, the seller offered to keep it hosted for free on his managed server for six months. The server ended up dying, and his web host (1&1 Internet) supposedly did not have a backup like they were supposed to, so I lost the site. The 2nd site did alright but was really not worth the trouble of running it, so I sold it in 2015 for $12,000. I also bought 50-100 small sites during 2005 and 2006, but none of them ended up being home runs. Many of the sites made significantly less than the seller's claimed, and it was a lot of trouble dealing with taking over the sites and moving them to my server (many times it would cause my server to crash, bringing down all my other sites also), so it turned out not to be worth it. Part of the problem is that although I know how to run sites, I am not good at promoting them, so I was not able to get additional traffic to any of the sites I purchased.

- **Dubious Business Deals** - In the late 1990s, I paid around $20,000 to buy a bunch of keywords in some sort of browser search plugin. I never received any traffic from it. A few years later, I paid a similar amount to a company to develop a downloadable toolbar for Bored.com. That never ended getting completed. Out of hundreds of dealings I have had over the years, most went fine, but after those big losses I was a lot more careful.

- **Bottlenecks** - In the 1990s and early 2000s, I should have outsourced more work. I always had a one to two year backlog of projects for my one full-time programmer. This was good, in that I never had to worry about having enough work to keep him employed, but bad because there were a lot of sites I could have launched much sooner if I had just been able to get them all done faster. Also, when I eventually expanded to have several different programmers (via outsourcing), I would keep up the pace and think of even more sites to build, so overall I was much more productive. Another issue was that the first programmer I ever hired (part-time, around 1997) cost $50/hr so I was hesitant to have him do too many projects for me. At that price, it was not always worth it. Later when I started hiring people at $10 an hour, that made it much less risky for me to spend a lot of programming time launching new sites.

- **Prepayments** - Many times I have prepaid people for projects, either to get a discount or just because that is what was required. More often than not, this does not work out. People almost always ask for more money for the next job before they finish whatever they were supposed to do.

- **Missed Opportunities** - I should have started creating mobile apps much sooner than I did. I was an early Blackberry user, but at that time Blackberry phones were mainly for email and were no good for surfing the web or for apps. I also was not on Facebook or Twitter. I understood the potential of social media, but because I was not a heavy user myself, I did not feel comfortable doing anything. I eventually switched to an iPhone and got the hang of things, but by then the app business and social media markets were much more crowded.

So, what did I learn from 20 years of mistakes? Every day in business is a learning experience, whether I win or lose. The Internet is constantly changing and what works well one year might totally bomb the next. And, what works best for me is not necessarily how other people should do things. There are many roads that lead to online wealth, and unlike in the traditional corporate 9-to-5 world, you should do things in the way that you are most comfortable. There is no one right way to run your business. Some people raise millions in venture capital, others start from their dorm room or garage. The important part is to always keep trying, to always keep thinking of new ways to make money, and to always keep dreaming about making it big.

How I Found My Voice

When I was in high school, I wasn't a typical teenager. I was not a geek, not a jock (playing on the tennis team did not count), and not popular. I was a shy, socially awkward, honor roll student, who read the *Wall Street Journal* every day in the school library during study hall.

Fast forward ten years later (1995), and I discovered the wonders of using the Internet. Instead of having to deal with people in person, I could do everything by phone or email, so I was in heaven. But, in the many years I spent working seven days a week, 16+ hours a day online building my company and buying thousands of domains, I was never really a consumer of what was out there. I did not take advantage of everything the Web had to offer. Sure, I looked at viral videos and went to silly websites, but I was just an anonymous person visiting faceless pages. Although I owned a bunch of popular websites (such as Bored.com), I always stayed in the background of the industry, doing my own thing. Bored.com was a reflection of my personality, and I put my heart into that site, but nobody cared who created or ran it. It just was.

All that changed significantly for me, however, in the late 2000s. After I sold half my websites (including Bored.com) in 2008, I took more time to try to learn about what everybody else was doing. I started reading a handful of blogs each day (TechCrunch.com, Domaining.com, JamesAltucher.com), news sites (TheDailyBeast.com, CNN.com, MarketWatch.com), and entertainment sites (TMZ.com, RadarOnline.com, Facebook.com). I also started to read ten times as many business books as I used to, mainly due to the convenience of being able to read them in e-book format on the Kindle I had just purchased.

(I now read them instead on my iPhone via the Kindle app.)

Around that same time, I realized that it was kind of pointless for me to have a company home page, as I stopped having clients in the late 1990s. Instead, I converted my ImpulseCorp.com website to be primarily a blog for my business. I was not sure what I was going to publish, but I figured I would come up with something. I made some interesting blog postings over the first few months, but it was not until I told the behind-the-scenes story of how I sold Bored.com that my blog started to get noticed.

Also during that time, I began writing songs. Up until age 38, I had no desire to be a songwriter and played no musical instruments. One day I happened to walk into a bookstore and see a book on sale for $8 called something like *Record Your Own Hip-Hop Song*, and it even came with a microphone and software, so I bought it. Within 24 hours, I had written and recorded my first song, and soon the floodgates opened. By the end of the year, I had recorded 50 songs, and now have almost 150. I even had a minor Internet hit with *Pimp My Sleigh*.

Up to this point, I was basically just expressing myself in new, more public ways. This year, though, I have been trying to actively become part of the overall feedback loop of life. For example, I joined a site called Criticue.com, where you view screenshots of websites and give webmasters your opinions about what you like and dislike, and any improvements you think they should make to the site. For each site you review, you get one credit towards a review of your own site. Many webmasters of the sites I reviewed messaged back to me right away with comments or questions, and some made my suggested changes. In addition, I appreciated hearing the comments I received, and I incorporated some of them on my sites.

I also joined an online forum for songwriters, where I critique the lyrics of songs that other songwriters post, and they review mine. For every song I post, I probably review at least 50 other songs. I have found that critiquing is like a muscle I flex, where the more I do it, the easier and stronger it gets. I like giving my opinion because I know the songwriters are eager to hear it. And, when people review my songs, it helps me improve as a songwriter.

Even more recently, I was asked by DomainInvesting.com (Elliot's Blog) to do some guest postings, and that has been going well. It helps me reach a much wider audience. I also have become more active posting comments on articles in domain-related blogs. I was even invited to be a keynote speaker at two different domain conferences, but I declined. It was flattering, but I really like to keep things as virtual as possible. I wouldn't have a problem with speaking to an audience of 1,000 people about a topic I feel comfortable with (domains); I just don't like to travel for business. I don't want to be away from my wife and kids, and I don't want to spend the time involved in preparing for it and traveling there and back. I would much rather be working. This is the same reason I have never attended any industry conferences or trade shows, and the same reason I love having a home office.

Some people experience the thrill of life through extreme sports, partying, dating, gambling, and the like. I have my biggest adventures online and am fine with that. I am still the same shy, quirky kid I was in high school. But different. I am a work in progress.

Epilogue

What's Next For Me?

While other teenagers were playing video games and watching sports, I was reading the *Business Week*, buying penny stock IPOs, and thinking of inventions. While other college kids were partying, I was starting student businesses and trying get-rich-quick schemes. While other graduates went off and got jobs, I bought rental properties, stayed up all night tinkering around on the Internet, and spent all my money on domain names. Then, as my business began to take off, I worked 16 hours a day, 7 days a week, for 20 years to try build it into an online empire. Through all this, my singular obsession in life was to make lots of money. It was my drive, my passion. It gave my life a sense of purpose. The question is, what do I do now?

Having money has made my life easier and less stressful, but I am not really any happier than I used to be. One reason for this is that I still am under pressure to make even more money. My plan had been to put the $3 million I made from selling Bored.com in the bank and live off the interest. But, with CD interest rates at only 1% right now, that income does not amount to much (especially after taxes). And, although I still have a large business left, it does not make a big profit like it used to.

By selling most of my sites, I traded my next 20-30 years worth of income for a lump-sum payment right now. The problem is that I am only 46 years old, and most people in my family have lived into their 90s, so I need to plan financially for the next 50 years. Although $3 million seems like a large amount of money, it won't last that long if I spend it to live on.

I still have a strong desire to become a business tycoon (like Bill Gates, Donald Trump, Warren Buffett, etc.), and I still constantly think of new business ideas, but things are not the same. My work day is filled with all the various tasks of running a business (paying bills, answering phone calls, handling website problems, dealing with workers, etc.), and I am not as motivated to take on new ventures. Everything seems less important now. Making changes or adding new content to my sites could at best make a few thousand dollars a year extra, but might also have no effect, so either way why bother? I feel like I should be spending my time on bigger things.

In the past, lack of funds kept me from starting many of the businesses that I conceived. Now that money is not as much of a problem, I am in a better position to start something new. No more financing things on credit cards at 25% interest rates, trying to get partners or investors, or worrying about cash flow problems. I would not even have the pressure of needing the business to make a profit right away. But, then I think about all the work involved in a startup and how in the end I might not even make anything from it (I could even lose money), and in comparison just living off my existing income does not seem like that bad an option. So for now I feel stuck. Being an entrepreneur and trying to get rich makes me happy, but I don't want to make my life full of stress and time pressures again as that will make me unhappy.

Some studies in the field of behavioral economics shed some light on this topic. Contrary to what you would expect, experiments show people are less happy when they have a lot of options. They often get overwhelmed and paralyzed by all the choices. For example, in an experiment set up by psychologists Mark Lepper and Sheena Iyengar, customers at a jam tasting booth in an upscale supermarket in California were ten times more likely to buy the jam when they were offered 6 varieties vs. 24 varieties. Or think about it this way instead: In his book *The Paradox of Choice: Why More Is Less*, Barry Schwartz gives the example of how in the olden days, when you walked into a clothing store to buy a pair of jeans, all you had to do was find your size and you would be done in five minutes. Now when you go to Gap, you can choose from a dozen different types (stonewashed, slim, acid-washed, distressed, boot cut, relaxed, taper, button-fly, skinny, etc.). Aside from all the extra time and mental energy it takes to pick the right jeans, you probably will walk out of the store less happy then when there was only one choice, because you will be thinking about all the other choices you could have made.

Everyone wants more. More money, more success, more power, more freedom. But, does that really lead to happiness? Research by happiness economists (no, I am not making that profession up) shows that as predicted, "good" things like a stable marriage, excellent health, and sufficient income make people happier, while "bad" things like unemployment, divorce, and economic instability make people less happy. But, contrary to popular belief, being rich does not lead to significantly more happiness than just having a moderate income. Studies show that one reason for this is that wealthy people spend less time doing what brings them pleasure, and more time doing compulsory things and feeling stressed. Plus, as shown in tabloid magazines and soap operas, rich people have a whole new world of problems to deal with such as fame, security issues, addictions, financial meltdowns, family pressures, and lawyers.

My own personal paradox is that even though the pursuit of money makes me happy, now that I have a sufficient amount of it, the research indicates making more money won't make me any happier. One solution would be to make more money but then give some of it away to charity (philanthropy generally makes people happy). Or, maybe I should expand my horizons and find other activities to enjoy such as travel, reading, volunteering, sports, religion, hobbies, video games, family, and all the other exciting things life has to offer.

So, I stand now at a crossroads. My future is full of opportunities. It is not time yet for me to slow down or retire. I want to make a difference in the world, do great things, and make my mark on history. I don't know what lies ahead or what path I will take, but I look forward to the journey.

www.ingramcontent.com/pod-product-compliance
Lightning Source LLC
Chambersburg PA
CBHW031048180526
45163CB00002BA/733